PROPERTY INVESTING MADE EASY

Achieve Financial Freedom in 6 Months

"Set a goal to achieve something that is so big, so exhilarating that it excites you and scares you at the same time." – Bob Proctor

Danny and Jo Phillips

With much success

Danny +

Jo x

10-10-10
Publishing

First published in 2018

ISBN-13: 978-1727772623
ISBN-10: 1727772628

www.phillipsrealestate.co.uk

Disclaimer
The authors assert that they cannot be held liable or responsible for the outcomes of decisions the reader makes as a result of reading this book. The reader is wholly responsible for their actions and should seek relevant professional advice before making any decision that may affect their business and life. We are not a financial advisory service. You should seek professional financial advice regarding any matters contained within this book and we are not liable for any financial decisions you make as a result of any content in this book. This book is for inspiration only and its contents are a reflection of the author's personal experience and should not be taken as advice.

Published by
10-10-10 Publishing
Markham, ON
Canada

Table of Contents

To Our Family

We dedicate this book to our four children, Ben, Carmella, David, and Sarena, and our nephew, Blade. We hope that this book is an inspiration to you all.

Foreword

If you are serious about buying your first investment property, then this book is a must-read. Get ready to feel empowered from the inspiration and motivation, and you will be able to apply this knowledge in your own life and business as you begin the journey to financial freedom.

You are certainly living in exciting times, where you can access the knowledge and understanding to become a property investor. Once you join the property investing world, you will begin to understand how you can achieve financial success by providing a professional service to your tenants and by creating the perfect win-win situation. Are you looking to start your own property portfolio? Are you looking for a life of wealth and abundance? Do you need to be inspired to transform your first steps into action? No matter who you are, or your background, your religion or culture, this book will give you the knowledge and insights to make property investing a reality.

I am delighted to endorse this book, *Property Investing Made Easy – Achieve Financial Freedom In 6 Months*. Authors Danny and Jo Phillips have taken on the mammoth industry of real estate investing, and have condensed it into simple bite-sized chunks for you to digest. Their lessons learned and their forward vision will ignite a spark in you to see your dreams become a reality.

Raymond Aaron
New York Times Bestselling Author

Testimonials

"This is an encouraging and uplifting read, brimming with tricks and tips for the new property investor. Danny and Jo are an inspiration for those just starting out in the property sector."
Darren Winters – Property Investor & Master Stock Market Trader

"I'm delighted in how my mentees have developed over the last 12 months. This book is a shining example of their devotion and perseverance. An honest and impressive read."
Kam Dovedi – Founder of Premier Property, Property Expert

"I first met Danny and Jo at an event I was speaking at, in April 2017. They were in the audience, nodding along to all I was saying, and then, before the end of the talk, they up and left! Little did I know that they'd left to get in a prime place to grab me after my talk. They took massive action that day, joined our Property Partner programme, and have been taking massive action, experiencing the highs and lows of property development and investing, ever since. I can think of no better accolade than that I know that they are perfectly positioned and qualified to be your guide through the first year of investing in property. They have lived, walked the talk, and earned this book. I'm proud to have played a small part in their success, and be assured that you are in good hands with this dynamic duo."
Alan Christie – Director Development Discovery, Expert Property Developer

"Congratulations and well done for your contributions in the property field. This book will be a great asset to those just starting out."
Pauline Heron – Director Development Discovery, Business Psychologist

"You're so inspirational! Great to see you growing as property investors, and as business people in general. Looking forward to reading the book!"
Eduardo Prato – Director Development Discovery, Property Management Consultant

"When it comes to property books, most of them either talk down to the reader or use technical jargons that raises more questions than they answer. Danny and Jo sit alongside the reader and share their personal and emotional story that actually helps the reader to learn about the industry and how to get started."
Charles Zhao - Director of Finance, Development Discovery, Angel Investor

Acknowledgements

We would first like to thanks Jo's parents, Bill and Chris Ogden, for all their love and support over the years, and for the encouragement that they have given to us to aspire to bigger and better things.

Thank you for the endless love and caring that you have both given to us, and for the wisdom that you have shared. We have learned so much from you, and I feel honoured to be your daughter.

We would also thank Sally Munden, Jo's sister, and Blade our nephew, for always being so encouraging and inspiring to us.

We would like to thank our four wonderful children: Ben, Carmella, David, and Sarena. You are all truly amazing people, and have grown up into wonderful, caring, and inspiring adults.

You are all achieving great things along your chosen paths, and this inspires us both daily.

We feel privileged to have you all in our lives, and grateful to you all for the love and affection that you give.

Chapter 1

Where Do I Start?

Start As You Mean to Go On

"The biggest risk is not taking any risk." – **Mark Zuckerberg**

Oh no, not another book about property! I hear ya! However, this book is different in so many ways. When we were starting out on our property journey, about this time last year, we were like rabbits in headlights. We had so much information given to us, so much free content available to advise us, but we had no idea what was good advice and what was not. If you feel like this, you are in the right place. Rest assured, we have written this book in a way that is EASY to read, and in a format that is EASY to digest and EASY to refer back to if necessary. This book isn't for people who are experienced or have large property portfolios. It is for those people who have been thinking that property is a good idea, but they just don't know how to get started. We are not claiming to be experts, but we feel that we can help and assist you on those first steps into your property journey in order to go from thinking about it to actually buying your very first piece of real estate.

The biggest thing we have learnt, through all the education we have had in these last 12 months, is to take action, stop procrastinating, stop thinking it through, and stop organising or waiting for all the ducks to be in a row or the stars to align—because they never will! Just do something today!

We began, just like you, by reading books. We read all kinds of property and investing books, using Audible. We gained so much valuable information; however, a lot of the books were too vast, and gave us so many different ways and different strategies of making money! Written by people who have had years and years in the *game,* these books were inspiring, yet made us overwhelmed and confused. We wanted to write a book that strips the information back to the basics so you can clearly see how to buy a good investment, how to avoid making mistakes, and how to move forward, step-by- step, and make property investing EASY.

If you are like us, chances are you have been considering buying property for over a number of years. We dabbled with the thoughts of being a landlord, and occasionally looked in the window of the local high street, at the estate agent's windows covered with glossy pictures of properties. By the time we had finished looking at the first picture, the inner critic had already started: *"Who do you think you are to own property? You are not the next Richard Branson, you know! You wouldn't know how to do it! If you did buy something, you would probably buy the wrong thing and lose a load of money anyway. It's not such a great time to buy property at the moment anyway... the market is probably going to turn."* And this is a good one: *"Why would we want phone calls at 2am, telling us that the toilet has broken and is overflowing!"* And why is it always 2 o'clock in the morning anyway? All these discouraging, unhelpful, and negative thoughts and beliefs, and that is only while we were viewing the properties in the window! We didn't even go in!! And so, we would walk on, shelving the entrepreneurial dream once more. It's easy to make excuses; but hopefully, this book will inspire you to see that you can do it: achieve success and income that can support your existing lifestyle, and give you the inspiration to achieve even more in years to come.

It's all too easy to just live in the rat race, working 9–5. Your boss tells you what to do, so you do it. You get paid at the end of the month, and then moan that you only have enough to pay for the bills, and little for anything else. You come home at the end of each day, and you're tired. All you want to do is take off your shoes, sit on the sofa, have a drink, watch some TV, and zone out—been there, done that, got the T-shirt, we hated it. There is another way! Let us show you how you can take charge of your life, your income, your finances, your dreams, and ultimately, your destiny. This is probably why you bought this book. It's not necessarily the love of real estate that has prompted you but the possibilities of what having regular passive income will do for you and your loved ones. So, congratulations on making the decision to change the whole of the rest of your life, starting right here, right now.

What is the biggest risk you've ever taken? Is it getting married? Was it buying a car, or maybe even your first home? It can be both exciting and very stressful making these decisions, but the question is, *why did you make them?* Maybe it was something that you've wanted to do for many years. Did you feel that it was a step in the right direction to achieve your goal? Only you know the real motivation behind why you made your decisions. So, our question to you is, *why do you want to invest in real estate now? What would the passive income do for you?* Stop and have a good think about it, as this exercise will help you progress through this book.

Now, as we go on, hold onto that thought and keep it at the forefront of your mind as we go through this book.

So, what has motivated us to be on this pathway, and has kept us going? We could simply say *financial freedom,* and that *failure is not an option*, and that's quite a positive mindset, I'm sure you'll agree. It would have been easy not to take the risk. Jo and I both receive pensions. We were both police officers in London, UK. I had served 35 years as a warranted officer, and Jo served 8 years. We could easily have continued our lives, living month to month, with this modest pension. Things would have been quite tight financially, but we would have struggled through. We would have eventually paid off our mortgage, and this may have freed up a little bit of money; however, if you factor in the cost of inflation, it wouldn't have given us very much more purchasing power.

We currently live in a two-bedroom apartment on the outskirts of London, and at some point, we would have had to move further outside London in order to free up some money to live on. But we wanted more—a lot more. We were not ready to hang up our hats just yet and settle for what life had given us. No! We decided to take the bull by the horns and create our own destiny. So, quite simply, staying where we were was not an option. We wanted to move forward and have the luxury lifestyle that we both wanted, living off a passive income that we had created. You can too!!

So now, having laid the foundation of our property portfolio we have achieved financial freedom. But it doesn't stop there. We are now aiming for financial luxury. This book is a concise guide for anyone thinking about property investment. We hope you enjoy this book as much as we have enjoyed writing it.

Work Out What You Want

"Real estate investing, even on a very small scale, remains a tried and true means of building an individual's cash flow and wealth."
– Robert Kiyosaki

Early on in our property education, we were advised to work out exactly what we want in life, and to set it as a goal for the future. This has been extremely helpful, and we suggest you do the same if you haven't already. We asked you previously what you really want out of property investing, and now is the time to look at it in more detail.

Remember to be specific when you are thinking about your goal. Make sure you set a deadline and a way that you can measure your success along the way. Some people in the property community use the

S.M.A.R.T goal system, and this is helpful:

S – Specific
M – Measurable
A – Achievable
R – Realistic
T – Timely

Some people like to get rid of the realistic and just make their goals BIG! We decided to do this! We have a goal of 200 properties in 5 years. I don't know how we are going to do it, and it scares us, but hey, we are in this for the long term, and if your goal doesn't scare you, then it's just not big enough!

Maybe you are looking at property investment as a vehicle to give you a pension income to supplement your government pension? Maybe you are looking at it as a new career choice? Maybe the income from property investing will give you the freedom to never have to work again. Neither Jo nor I want to have to work and have a job. We want our property investing to give us the income to achieve our other goals in life. Maybe you want the property income money to allow you to travel the world. Or maybe to start your own business or support an ever expanding family. The main thing to remember is that everyone is different, and that there is no right or wrong goal.

Spend a few moments now, thinking about what your goal is. *If you had all the money in the world and never had to work ever again, what would you do with your life? What has been your passion since you were a child? What are you really good at? What makes you happy and brings you the greatest joy in life?*

If you find this hard to answer right now, it might be a good idea to gain a different perspective and to go and ask your family and friends for their opinions.

It is important to voice or write down what you really want out of life. It is all too easy to fall into the trap of doing what is expected of you by society or what your parents wanted for you. Our school system is like a conveyor belt in a sausage factory, telling people what they should know in order to get employment in a job. Robert Kiyosaki says that having a JOB stands for Just Over Broke, as do many others in the property investing circles. The expected social norm of life in the Western world would be to go to school, get a job, have a family, retire, and die. Have you ever questioned your existence or the fact that you are the master of your own life? If you conform and are employed, there will always be a ceiling to the amount of money that you can earn or save. By having your own business, and/or being an investor, it gives you the freedom to live life on your terms, and not have someone else dictate to you how much money that you can make. We would highly recommend that you also read *The Cashflow Quadrant,* by Robert Kiyosaki, for more insight, and to see how this works.

You are the creator of your own destiny. You have the power inside you to choose your own path in life—where you live, your friends, how to spend your day. Ultimately, you have control over everything—what you eat, what you wear, and what you say.

Maybe you want to write your own book. You can do it! Maybe you want to have a big family. You can do it!! You might want to own the latest Porsche or Tesla. You can do it. Once you have declared what you really want for your life, we suggest writing it on a piece of paper and looking at it and reading it out loud as motivation every day. Some people use a vision board to propel them on their journey to getting exactly what they want.

If you don't discover exactly what you want in life, then you are destined to be like tumbleweed in the desert, being pushed from one side to the other as the wind blows, with no direction or purpose. You may know people like this in your own life.

This chapter may have opened your eyes to the monotony and lack of direction in your own life. This can only ever be a good thing, because now, you cannot *unsee* what you have seen, and you won't be able to go back without an aching in your gut that will compel you to strive forward and to get what you really want from life.

We will advise you on how to achieve these goals later in the book, but for now, just dream... dream BIG!

Setting Your Goals

"To know what you know and what you do not know,
that is true knowledge."
– Confucius

The most fundamental key to success is goal setting. It's a way of creating your future in words or pictures before it actually happens.

So, by now, you will have your goal, and an idea of when you want to achieve this by. You know the phrase... *How do you eat an elephant? One bite at a time.* It is the same for any goal. Your goal may seem daunting, overwhelming, and too big. This is a good thing! Ours is too!

One of our dreams is to own a large, detached property with 5 bedrooms. It would have a place where Jo can do her arts and crafts and all her creative stuff, an office, and a gorgeous country kitchen, and be set in a substantial garden of 1–2 acres, with rolling hills for scenery. This would be a gated property, with electronic access gates for security, and a drive in and out pebbled driveway leading up to the house. There would be an electric double garage and enough space for our Tesla and Bentley. We would have a swimming pool and spa bubble pool, with a gym at the side of the house, with showering and changing facilities. We would have a cleaner, a cook, someone who comes to wash our cars, and also a gardener.

We would love to be able to travel in comfort wherever we want, whenever we want, in luxury rather than being stuffed into economy, and to be able to stay at luxury 5*+ hotels, anywhere in the world. We want to have enough time in our lives to spend with our family and future grandchildren, and have them come and stay at the house.

We want to have all of this and to have enough passive income surplus for enjoying and investing. A passive income is money that comes in that you do not have to work for. So, instead of working for money, and getting paid at the end of the month, every month, you work upfront for a few months, then get paid FOREVER!! It is important that any goal you set will motivate you. There is no point in setting goals that you will find boring or things that you feel that you have to do.

Ask yourself why this goal is important and valuable to you. By writing down your goals, something magical happens, by giving you a tangible end point. It is best to write your goal out in the present tense, rather than, for example, *"I really want,"* or *"I would like."* Here is an example of one of our goals written down:

So, let's take Danny's worthy idea of training first aid using the S.M.A.R.T goals theory. *Between now and (specific date) I have achieved earnings of £50,000.00 per month and in return for the money I will provide fantastic first aid training services all over the UK in order to save lives and help people.* So, by writing out this goal, we have been specific about the amount of money we want. We can measure our success by having received that money. It is achievable through property investing and reinvesting this money into FAB Training our first aid company. It is relevant, as we want to upgrade our lifestyle. It is timely because we have written a specific date to achieve this by.

These are just a couple of examples of our dreams and goals through property investment. When we started we had a goal of 20 properties, we soon realised that this wouldn't be real enough to achieve the luxurious lifestyle we desire. Having read a book by Grant Cardone, called *The 10X Rule*, we have simply multiplied our goal by 10, and now have a goal of 200 properties. You will need to work out how many properties in your goldmine area that you need to purchase in order to fund the dreams, goals, and lifestyle that you really want and desire. It might seem overwhelming right now, but this book will show you how to buy your first property investment; and after that, you just copy and paste the system until you achieve your goals—by which time you may have bigger goals.

It is a good idea to revisit your goals either half yearly or every three months. We have written our goals in a computer document and can amend and update the goals when we come to review. We suggest making a date in your diary for revisiting your goals. It is all too easy to get busy with other things and forget the reason behind what you are doing and what you want to achieve. By having a dedicated hour in your diary, you allow yourself time to focus on you and your personal development.

Use this time to celebrate the successes, and to acknowledge your efforts, if you have been working towards your goal. Keep a record of your achievements, no matter how small. Be completely honest with yourself if you haven't been working on your goals— don't be harsh on yourself, but use the time to find out why, and ask yourself how you are willing to change. If you have a close friend or partner that you are able to confide in, ask them if they would be willing to be your accountability partner. Ask them if they would be happy for you to text them, say every Sunday evening, to let them know your successes for the last week. This will help you be more accountable in seeing how you are progressing and achieving your goals. So, put a recurring appointment into your diary, and stick to it.

Mindset is Everything

"There is one quality which one must possess to win, and that is definiteness of purpose, the knowledge of what one wants, and a burning desire to possess it."
– Napoleon Hill

We suggest that before you even look at a property, you should get your head straight. It's great when things are going well, but it's all too easy to give up when something difficult comes along. Therefore, if you have your mindset primed beforehand, you will be able to withstand the difficult times, and you will come out stronger! We have learnt that if you fill your mind with positivity and have a good attitude about life, then you will attract good things into your life. One way we find helpful to do this is to follow motivational and inspirational Instagram pages. Every morning, we spend a few minutes soaking up the *Can-do* attitudes. Here are a few we love:

- Problems are opportunities.
- Life is not about waiting for the storm to pass but learning to dance in the rain.
- Believe you can and you're halfway there.
- Start each day with a grateful heart.
- All our dreams can come true if we have the courage to pursue them.
- Wake up each morning with the thought that something wonderful is going to happen.
- The secret of getting ahead is getting started.
- Choose to be positive. It feels better!
- Life has no remote. Get up and change it yourself.
- Let go of the thoughts that don't make you strong.

Now, Instagram may not be your thing. Another idea we use is to type the words out in Microsoft Word, and to put them round the house. We have ours by the kettle, computer, and bedside table. Make them short enough to absorb in an instant. We're not suggesting you read Hamlet while making a cup of tea! The idea is to fill your mind with good and positive stuff. We don't know the science behind it. We are not psychologists! We don't have to be, and neither do you. All we know is that it works. Affirmations are another great idea—writing down things that you want your self to be. Here are some that you can borrow from us:

- I am a positive person.
- I am wealthy.
- I am happy.
- I am healthy.
- I am full of energy.
- I am powerful.
- I am fierce.
- I am passionate.
- I am strong.
- I am loving.

Give it a go.

Do it now. Read through the list, saying each one 3 times. We suggest you find a calm place, away from the hustle and bustle of daily life, and just read them aloud slowly. Believe them, feel them, and absorb them! Do you feel empowered? We do! This is why we do it. It sets us up to power through the difficulties and obstacles that come our way. We are sure that it will work for you too. If you would like to, feel free to write to us, at www.phillipsrealestate.co.uk/book, and tell us how your mindset is changing and developing. You can also print off some affirmations for yourself, which we have prepared especially for you.

Having a positive mindset is essential to the property investor. We all know those people who are always negative, and those that have a positive outlook on life in general. We do believe that optimism is something that can be learnt—we try to catch ourselves if we are being negative, and try to put a positive spin on it. We have seen a difference in our lives by making these changes. Where attention goes, energy flows; and if it is positive energy, then all the better.

The movie, *The Secret,* by Rhonda Byrne, which is also now in book format, explains that the secret is the universal law of attraction. It explains, in documentary form, how philosophers, authors, scientists, geniuses, and other significant influential people all understood how the law of attraction works. We, too, can apply this great secret into our own lives in order to achieve everything that we want in life. In the movie, you see several famous people all giving an account of how they used the secret in their own lives, in respect to every aspect of life, including relationships, health, wealth, and happiness. We highly recommend watching the movie. You will begin to see how the law of attraction has been working in your life thus far, whether for good or bad. One of the examples given is if you continuously think and worry about debt, even if you are trying to avoid it, you will attract debt. If you can shift your mindset to think about prosperity, then you will receive prosperity from the Universe.

Here are some brilliant quotes by T. Harv Eker, which will get you thinking about your own mindset:

"Rich people believe, 'I create my life.' Poor people believe,
'Life happens to me.'"
"Rich people are committed to being rich.
Poor people want to be rich."
"Rich people focus on opportunities. Poor people focus on obstacles."
"Rich people associate with positive, successful people. Poor people
associate with negative and unsuccessful people."
"Rich people act in spite of fear. Poor people let fear stop them."

So, by having a positive mindset when you embark on your property journey, you will be able to take risks, face fears, and overcome obstacles so much easier than before. By taking the time to work on your personal development, you will withstand the storms, the trials, and the difficulties, as you progress through this huge learning curve of property investment.

Jump In With Both Feet

"The path to success is to take massive, determined actions."
– Tony Robbins

We are not suggesting we know it all. Far from it. But we know a heck of a lot more than we did 12 months ago, and we would like to share that knowledge with you.

So, a bit about us… We met in Starbucks, in Golders Green, London, UK, 18 years ago. I was a police officer at the time, and Jo was working at John Lewis department store, London, UK, in the Gift List department for weddings and bar mitzvahs. I encouraged Jo to join the police, and over the next few years, she did. We lived in Barnet, in London, in Jo's apartment, before buying our first house together in Harrow, in London. Our first ever property was a semi-detached house with 3 bedrooms, a lounge, and a kitchen at the back. There was a garage to the side and a garden to the rear. It was in need of some love and attention (code words for very old fashioned and unmodern!). We hired some builders, got planning permission from the local authority, and moved into Danny's parents' house while the renovation was being done. Just as the project was being finished, Jo was forced to be medically retired from the police, due to a medical condition called Ehlers-Danlos syndrome hypermobility type. It was causing Jo too much pain, and she was unable to work as a police officer. We were gutted. Due to the lack of income and not being able to meet our monthly mortgage payments, we reluctantly sold our lovely dream house that had been done out just as we had planned.

We moved to Radlett in Hertfordshire, a small village just outside London. The house was half the size of the previous one, and in need of that *love and attention* again. We were back to square one. Well, maybe even two steps back! Jo decided to start her own business, where she would be working for herself at a pace that would suit her disability. *Jowish* was born. Together, we started *Jowish*, a Jewish greeting card company. Jo had dreamt about having her own designs on greeting cards since she was young, and now that she had completed her Masters in Illustration, she had the drive to start up her own company. Jowish really took off, but we found ourselves absorbed in yet another job. Jo was working hard, and was becoming very stressed again. Our goal was to get these Jewish greeting cards into John Lewis, where Jo had worked previously. We achieved this within 3 years, and we were delighted. However, due to the time it took up, the stress of it, and our lack of knowledge of business, we decided to sell the company to a competitor.

During these last 3 years, we *tarted up* our 2-up, 2-down house in Radlett. We did not have the funds for a complete refurbishment project, and having looked at the ceiling price for the road, decided to just repaint and carpet instead. We put the property on the market and sold again—this time making a healthy profit! We were over the moon, as this gave us more purchasing power. We then moved into our current home.

Again, this apartment was in need of some love and attention. It was a probate property, and so we were able to buy it below market value. Jo could see past the dated, soft peach-coloured walls, and the green and red speck carpets. The green bath and the flowery green and peach curtains bothered her not. Danny was unable to see past this horrible decoration but trusted Jo on the purchase, as Danny had seen that she had revamped the previous three places—and he had faith in her.

This property is an 1840s mansion, divided into 12 apartments, situated in Bushey, another small village on the outskirts of London. This refurb was more difficult, as we decided to stay in the flat while the works were being carried out. It was difficult for us both, and for Snuggles, our cat, living in a building site with dust everywhere! Never again! It took about 4 months to finish the project, and it now looks great! Five years down the line, and the valuation is that it has nearly doubled!

As you can see, property has always been on our minds, and renovations have been our thing, so far. Property investment has been something we have wanted to do for a long time. We knew that property was a good investment for the long term, and that property prices eventually go up over time, and that a steady stream of rental income would be great. However, we worried about buying the wrong property, in the wrong area, and not getting tenants, or having tenants that would trash the place. So our thoughts and dreams never went any further than that.

It was really only at the beginning of January 2017 that we took the bull by the horns, and decided to get educated. I would be retiring in May 2017, and would receive a healthy lump sum from my pension at the police. Firstly, we read a book that many of you may have already read: *Rich Dad Poor Dad*, by Robert Kiyosaki. Jo's sister, Sally, had been telling her to read it for years, and it had fallen onto deaf ears until January 2017, when everything changed. We bought the book, and Jo read it quickly on Audio Books! After reading it, Jo had what she can only describe as a financial awakening. Jo immediately suggested that I read it, which I did, and now we are telling everyone to read it. If you haven't read it, we suggest you put this book down and read that one first! The biggest lesson in the book for us was learning the difference between an asset and a liability. Robert says an asset is something that puts money into your pocket, and a liability is something that takes money out of your pocket. If you haven't read *Rich Dad Poor Dad*, you are missing out! What a fantastic book! This book has sold, worldwide, over 26 million copies to date. It is a real eye opener, and a jaw dropping book that shows us the matrix we are living in! This book recommendation is a foundation for your property journey, so go and get a copy if you haven't got one! And if you have, then you know what we're talking about. Robert, along with his wife Kim, also hosts a podcast, if you are interested in following them.

When we began to think of our home as a liability, and the fact that we owned NO ASSETS at all, we knew something had to change! We immediately signed up for a course with *Rich Dad,* and began our educational journey. We jumped right in, and we wished we had done it years ago.

Taking Action Today

"Knowledge is the treasure, but practice is the key to it." **– Lao Tzu**

At the beginning of our journey, we attended a *Rich Dad Poor Dad Cashflow* meetup group, in Central London. *Cashflow* is a board game created by Robert and Kim Kiyosaki. The purpose of the game is to educate you about finances and getting out of the *rat race.* This board game has proved so incredibly popular that there are meetup groups who play together all over the world. We loved our first game, as it inspired us to learn more about money, what it really is, how it works, and how to take action. By attending these *cashflow* meetups, we soon understood the importance of how cash flow is *king* when it comes to property investment. Once we understood this concept, we began to take action.

It can be really easy to make excuses as to why you don't start your property journey: *I am too busy; I've got no money; the kids need me right now; I've got too much housework; the house is a mess; work takes up all of my time; I need to rest; I'm tired.* Is this you?

A lot of people say that they haven't got the time to devote to becoming a property investor. We have seen this over and over, where people will talk about investing, but there is no action. If you have a full time job, it is a lot more difficult. If you have kids, or you are looking after someone, as a caretaker on top of your job, then it can be even more difficult. Property investing takes time and will eat into your hours. A great way to increase your time is to get up 1 hour earlier each day, and use this time to focus on property investing. You could start with getting up 30 minutes earlier for the first few weeks, and increase this to 45 minutes, until you feel comfortable to achieve a whole hour. Or why not consider taking a cut in your hours at work. You may not see a return on your investment of time initially; however, the accumulative effect will produce a passive income that will give you back the money you initially took as a cut, and more.

The most important thing, when you get started in property, is to become educated in property investing. Remember: *"I believe the more I invest in myself and real education, the wealthier I become."* – Darren Winters

We think that once you have decided in your mind to become a property investor, you need to get educated before jumping in and buying something. So, before you even log into Google to do a property search, I would spend the next month at least getting educated. If you are working full time, then take even longer. It is better to learn from other people's mistakes early on, rather than making those mistakes yourself. If you jump in and buy a property now, without first learning what to buy and how to buy it, you could end up losing a lot of money, and having a liability on your hands. When you are just starting out, good education is the key.

Here are some suggestions that you could do to educate yourself:

- Read books
- Podcasts
- Join Facebook groups
- Webinars
- Seminars
- Audiobooks

- Meetup groups
- Networking events
- Property courses
- Mentorship
- Property magazines
- YouTube videos

The most valuable thing that we feel you should invest in is to get a good mentor; and we will explain exactly how a mentor can help you in your property journey in the next chapter.

Chapter 2

Education, Education, Education

Mentorship is Key

"An investment in knowledge pays the best interest."
– **Benjamin Franklin**

Getting a mentor, early on, will save you so much money and time in the long run. A mentor is a trusted and experienced advisor that will help you learn quickly, often from their mistakes and experiences, guiding you and holding your hand. Although this book is teaching you the basics, when you have questions, your mentor will be available to answer your questions and concerns, and give you the reassurance and encouragement if you are on the right path, and correct you if not. Like anything in life—if you want to get good in life—it's the same in property.

There are several people and companies out there that could mentor you. It is a matter of finding someone that you *click* with and can trust 100%. You need to be able to be open and to share with your mentor your thoughts, fears, and concerns, and not to think that you will be judged for asking a silly question, or feel that you should know the answer.

A good mentor will encourage and support you through good times and bad. They will help you reflect on your circumstances, give you their expert opinion, and then help you to come to your own conclusions and decisions. One of our mentors is Kam Dovedi, from Premier Property, who has been buying property investments for nearly 30 years. Kam has seen the ups and downs in the UK property market. We initially met Kam at the Excel Exhibition Centre, in London, at a Property Investment event, where he was presenting on stage about property investments. After this presentation, we spoke to Kam briefly, and felt an immediate connection. We were invited to a 1-day seminar, where Kam taught us the basics of property investing. This encouraged us to join his mentoring programme, where we meet with Kam on a one-to-one basis, once a month for an hour, to talk through our own projects and issues.

Part of the mentorship is a monthly meetup Mastermind Day. During this day, we meet up with other likeminded people who are part of the Premier Property Inner Circle. The day consists of us all being updated by each other regarding how the property market is changing in our specific goldmine areas. Kam usually then has a practical exercise for us all to do; for example, exploring our goals and dreams, and how realistically we are going to achieve this over a particular time scale. There is often an external expert speaker from within the property investing community, like tax advisors, interior designers, etc. Lunch is always provided, and this gives us an opportunity for networking with our peers. The day is often topped off by going out for a meal at a local restaurant.

Premier Property additionally holds several monthly evening events throughout different UK locations, where an expert speaker will give a talk, with an opportunity for questions after. These networking events maintain and sustain high energy and enthusiasm during the property journey, and are free to those people who have signed up to Kam's mentorship. At Christmas time, Premier Property holds a charity Christmas Ball. Last year, 2017, we won the award for *Fastest Newcomer to Property*, having purchased 4 properties in 4 months. We were delighted to receive such an accolade. Our award, a glass trophy, sits proudly on our mantelpiece in our lounge.

One of the exercises that we have done with Kam to stay accountable is by pairing up with an Inner Circle member. This works by agreeing to complete 3 goals each by a particular date, and to phone the person to check their achievements. Kam also asks us to stay accountable to him by texting weekly, one or more successes in property for that week. For example, we viewed 10 properties, read a particular property-related book, or made an offer on a prospective purchase of a property.

Once a month, we have the opportunity to send in a particular deal that we are considering. If your deal gets chosen, it may be featured on the monthly webinar deal clinic. Here, Kam will analyze, scrutinise, and dissect the proposal to see if it is a good deal or not. By seeing how Kam analyses the deals each month, it gives us the confidence to copy his direction on our own projects.

At the same Excel Exhibition in London, we attended another seminar about Houses in Multiple Occupation (HMO), run by a company called Development Discovery. We had heard of this phrase before, and were told that this type of rental property gives very high yields. This attracted us to listen further to the seminar. The seminar gave us an insight into this type of investment, and we came to realise the pitfalls of investing on your own without support. At the end of their public pitch, we spoke to them further and decided to join their mentorship programme, and spoke to Alan Christie, who is a co-director in the company.

Development Discovery (DD) has a wealth of property investing experience, from managing letting agencies to simple buy-to-lets, through to large developments of housing estates. Having this team of people, with a vast array of skills, gives us a wealth of knowledge to tap into. Development Discovery has supplied us with documents, spreadsheets, and an Excel formula document, where we input all of the figures. It takes into account the cost of the property, the cost of builders, and the cost of management. At the end, it tells you whether there's a suitable deal, whether there's any party money, and basically, whether this project would work and be profitable. This document would then be analysed and tweaked, and then, if it's viable, a member of the senior team would then visit the venue and confirm all the details stack up. Having a great builder with experience of HMOs is essential. Also, having a Chartered RICS Surveyor, who can advise you what the full commercial value would be when the building is fully occupied, is also vital.

Our monthly meetings give us the opportunity to ask burning questions, in a safe environment with our peers. We are able to update the group with our progress for the month, and this gives us an accountability, which keeps us on our toes. We are also kept accountable via a weekly electronic survey. This highlights how well we have been doing, what we can improve, and how we can think of different or more creative ways to think about a problem or issue.

As a mentee, we have access to DD's extensive educational library via their website. This includes videos and access to a large range of property e-learning educational subjects.

If you don't have a mentor, it's easy to make costly mistakes. Most of our mentors have made these mistakes already. We want to minimise our financial losses, and jumpstart our knowledge by having a mentor. This will give us the best chance of success in our property investment company.

Audiobooks are Fantastic

"Don't exchange time for money; exchange time for knowledge."
– Rob Moore

Jo struggled with reading from a very young age. When she was about 6 years old, she remembers standing at the teacher's desk, almost hyperventilating while reading out loud. She felt so self-conscious, and ashamed that she couldn't do what her other classmates could do. She couldn't seem to keep up. She used to dread reading a book to her parents, and grew up hating reading. When she was about 8 years old, she became very good friends with a girl named Amy, who was an excellent reader. Amy happily read the school books to Jo, up to the age of about 16. Jo scraped by in her English exams with a C, and it was only when she was at university, at the age of 18, that she was identified as having dyslexia. Having this title made her feel stupid; but slowly, over the years, she came to realise that it is just a different way of thinking and learning. Jo was advised by the university educational learning coordinator to read as many books as she could. The theory was that the more she read, the better she would become at reading. The fact was that when she read, she found it a real effort, and she wasn't able to follow any story or regurgitate any of the information that she was reading. The words on the page moved about, and she would see patterns in these words, which was distracting and confusing. The bottom line was that she was studying *art*, and she found reading art history books very boring, so Jo gave up reading unless she absolutely had to.

Jo had never used audiobooks for learning. Jo remembers having a tape cassette of the Alice in Wonderland story that she used to listen to as a child. She would listen to this over and over, but she never connected the dots to her dyslexia. Since becoming a property investor, audiobooks have been promoted to us as a way to absorb information quickly. We thought we would give this a go, and signed up for the free, 30- day trial by Audible. This has been a revelation, and it has completely changed how we both learn. From going from maybe having read 1 book a year in Jo's adult life, Jo has now read over 40 books in the last year, on Audible. We both can't get enough of it. Another great thing is that you can speed up the reader, from x1 speed to either 1.25 or 1.5 times speed or more, in order to leverage your time. Also, when you are reading a book, reading is all that you can do. However, audiobooks gives you the flexibility to listen whilst driving, exercising, cooking, or many other activities, which, again, is a fantastic leverage of time.

Our mentors often share book titles that they have found helpful, which in turn excels our knowledge. Not only do we recommend other property investing book titles—such as *Multiple Streams of Property Income,* by Rob Moore; *Rich Dad, Poor Dad*, by Robert Kiyosaki; *The Real Book of Real Estate*, by Robert Kiyosaki—but also books about changing your mindset. These books have been invaluable learning for us both. We try to put into practice some of the lessons that we learn from such books, and have seen positive results in our lives. Simple and creative ideas, such as thinking about your beliefs, changing any negative ones into positives, and reading them aloud every morning. These new beliefs soon stick, and your whole outlook on life can be changed.

Another idea we were introduced to was to feel the fear and do it anyway. In *Eat That Frog*, by Brian Tracy, the idea is to take the most difficult problem that you need solving, and to just get on and do it, and stop procrastinating. In the *Cashflow Quadrant*, by Robert Kiyosaki, he cleverly divides jobs and self-employment on one side, and business and investment on another. Most of us grow up being told to go to school, get a job, and save for the long term. Robert exposes how this way of thinking can keep you stuck and vulnerable in your life, and encourages the readers to create businesses and to make sound investments, especially in property.

Another amazing book available on Audible is *Think and Grow Rich* by Napoleon Hill. Napoleon spent twenty years studying over five hundred extremely successful individuals. He discloses the secrets to success and gives practical exercises for self-development towards success. In *Learned Optimism*, by Martin Seligman. Martin explains that although a person may have a personality of being optimistic or pessimistic, they can improve their optimism and even change from being a pessimist to an optimist. It is all too easy to believe that you are born a certain way, and that through difficult times and tragedy, life has made you a pessimist. Martin has given us the freedom and belief to know that we can change. In *You Were Born Rich* by Bob Proctor you are invited to join the audience of the three day seminar where Bob and the team give you practical steps for achieving your worthy life goals.

Podcasts, in a similar vein, are a fantastic learning opportunity, and we highly recommend Robert's *Rich Dad Radio Show* podcast, and Rob Moore's *the Disruptive Entrepreneur* podcast, just to get you started. A podcast is an episodic digital recording of audio and/or video that you can download and listen to whenever, or wherever, you like. Audiobooks give you great knowledge and, as we know, knowledge is power. It is only when we expand our knowledge and our minds that we can become better than we have ever been before.

Learning From Mistakes

"You don't learn to walk by following rules.
You learn by doing, and by falling over."
– Richard Branson

If you are anything like us, you will have been told that making mistakes is a bad thing. This is something that we have been brought up with in our school education, and at home. Taking exams, for example. If you fail a specific, important exam, we were told that we wouldn't be able to get the job that we wanted, which implied that we would fail to achieve in society. Failure and mistakes are not encouraged in school. If a child makes a mistake, they are often shamed in front of their peers, as an example of what not to do or how not to behave.

Although no one likes making mistakes, sometimes they turn out for the best. Take the Post-it note for example. The inventor, Spencer Silver, was looking to make a strong adhesive. While he was trying to create this, he actually made a substance that was significantly weaker than which already existed. It would stick to surfaces but could easily be pulled off again. It was only a number of years later, when a colleague of his used the adhesive on small bits of paper to mark the place in his hymn book, that the Post-it note was born.

It has only really been since embracing the property journey that we have come to realise that mistakes are OK. It is how we learn and grow as human beings. Richard Branson is right when he talks about a child learning to walk. The child does not just give up and say, "Well, that's it; I've tried once or twice. I can't do it." Indeed, the child gets up, falls down, gets up, falls down, over and over, until the time that he gets the hang of it. It then becomes second nature. It's the same as learning how to ride a bike. No one is born being able to ride a bike perfectly. In fact, most of us who tried to ride a bike, initially, fell to the ground. It was only by getting back up that we finally learnt how to ride a bike.

When we first started out, we were advised by well-meaning people not to wait to get into property, but to get into property, then wait. So we did. This implied that property prices always go up and, therefore, if we got in now, we would be financially better off— as property prices rise, we would make a gain in the equity.

We found a property in Manchester, UK, which had fantastic potential for it to be turned into 3 properties (two 2-bedroom houses, and 1 studio apartment). We thought that the price was fantastic. We had done some research and had comparable prices. We believed that we could achieve almost double our purchase price once the refurbishment was complete, by splitting the properties, revaluing the properties, and getting mortgages on all 3. The catch was that we needed to buy the property in cash. We didn't question this at the time and went ahead with the purchase. We were nervous about the purchase, but our excitement about being property investors negated our fears, and we jumped right in. At the time, we knew very little about property. We weren't educated, and we certainly weren't aware of the legalities of the purchase or intricacies of the splitting of titles.

We were recommended a builder by the agent selling the property, and having visited a property that he was currently refurbishing, we signed a contract with him for the 3 refurbishments.

It wasn't long before we realised that the quality of the workmanship was poor, and the time that it was taking was far too long. The communication with the builder became strained, and although we had given the builder the majority of the contracted money, we had only received 2 half-finished houses, and the basement was barely touched. It also turned out that the property that he was refurbishing, which we had been to see, was in fact his own house. We felt let down, disheartened, and angry. So, having sacked the first builder, we took on a second builder. This builder was initially great and very keen to help us, but we were soon in a position of unfinished promises and unfinished work. This time, we were not even able to speak or communicate with him. Frustrated and annoyed, we asked him to return the keys. It was only when the managing agent found that the keys had been posted through the letter box in the property, that we knew we had finished working with him. This project took over 6 months, and the letting agent was kind enough to organise a handyman to finish off the remaining works and snags.

Why are we telling you this? Because we don't want you to make the same mistakes as we have. In fact, many mentors in property have made similar or bigger mistakes than this. Some people will have made these kind of mistakes and come to the conclusion that property investment is not for them. We don't see it that way. We see these mistakes as a learning curve. We are in it for the long run. In saying that, however, hindsight is a wonderful thing, and if we would have had our time over again, there is no way that we would have bought this property.

What did we learn? We learnt that we should have got ourselves educated before buying our first property. We learnt not to give a builder money up front. Only pay him when he has finished up to a certain agreed stage of the build. Any requests to purchase large items or materials should be paid for directly to the supplier. We also learnt the difficulties of splitting a title, and have now been advised in our situation that a title split would prove too complicated for this property. We have learnt not to jump into complicated property deals when you are just starting out, and we would advise you to leave such complicated deals to the more experienced property investor, or until you are one yourself. We suggest that you stick to simple buy-to-let, single family homes or apartments that require minimal refurbishment attention, so that your property is let out quickly and you can start receiving cash flow for your next deal.

Transformational Courses

*"Your greatness is limited only by the investments
you make in yourself."*
– Grant Cardone

We have attended a number of courses during our first year. Free and paid courses will open your mind to what is out there. We signed up for a 1-day course with Premier Property. Most people at this course were new to property investment, and we were all in the same boat. Kam explained the history of the property market in the UK. He explained how he uses debt in order to buy more property, and how to buy properties at a discount and/or below market value. We were delighted with the amount of knowledge that was provided. We felt enthused, motivated, and encouraged, which gave us a thirst to learn more. So, it was here that we decided to sign up for the 3-day Premier Property Masterclass. This course was fantastic. Each day built on the previous day's knowledge. It was well designed, informative, and packed with easy to understand information. The core purpose of the 3 days was to change new investors into professional property investors. Kam gave us practical exercises to complete during the day, which were attainable and measurable. He showed us what to buy, where to buy, and how to buy. He showed us the process from start to finish of how to buy property, and explained the practicalities of getting a good refurbishment team. He explained how to add value to your property investment, and the different types of property investing avenues that are available. This included serviced accommodation, HMOs (houses of multiple occupation), rent-to-rent, buy-to-let, and how to succeed with joint ventures. Kam taught us that we can source properties, and package them for other property investors as a way to build the capital for our first investment, if you have no initial capital. One of our favourite parts of the whole 3 days was talking about estate agents. Kam explained in detail the different types of estate agent profiles that we may encounter, and we did some practical roleplays, which gave us more confidence in speaking to estate agents. This was both funny and very true. We were also encouraged to each stand up in turn and introduce ourselves, saying, *"Hello, my name is Danny, and I am a property investor."*

It might sound silly, but the change in mindset for us has been transformational. It gave us the confidence, when speaking to other people at networking events, to be able to introduce ourselves with pride and professionalism. A byproduct of the course was making friends with other people who were also on our learning level, and also people who were already property investors who were looking for fresh ideas. We highly recommend this 3-day course, and wish we had done it at the very beginning. Kevin Green, Rob Moore, Vincent Tan, and many others have similar courses, but they don't all need to be done at once. By listening to different teachers, you gain different perspectives, and creative ideas.

The HMO course that we signed up to with Development Discovery has been fantastic, and each Mastermind Day has given us new insights and great learning. Bouncing ideas with other mentees has been invaluable, and the support and encouragement that we get from all the DD team members has kept us going. The great thing about doing such a course is having experienced teachers to hold your hand through the learning process, knowing that you can ask lots of questions and not fear that you are going to be judged for not knowing something.

Another great reason to attend an organised course like this is to know that you will be avoiding the large pitfalls, by having experienced people to advise you. It can be financially crippling, and even cause you to break, if you invest in projects that you don't have sufficient knowledge in. Some of these courses can initially seem expensive; however, the wealth of knowledge and support that you can gain far outweighs these costs—and remember that they are all tax deductible and can be offset against your income for your business. Please speak to your financial advisor to get the best advice regarding your personal financial circumstances.

The best investment that you can make is in yourself and your knowledge and learning. It is never a waste of money!

Exhibitions, Seminars & Webinars

"I believe that if you have the right knowledge then it is easy and fun to make a lot of money"
– Darren Winters

The very first property exhibition show that we went to was at Excel London, in April 2017. It was a massive warehouse that had hundreds of companies with their own stands. Each stand had people who were eager to give you information, literature, and sweeties to entice you to come over and chat with them! They were there to promote their company and to get you to sign up to their product or service.

As we walked in, we were greeted by a chap from the RLA. This stands for Residential Landlords Association. The RLA is a membership association that is an expert in its field, giving current and up to date landlord and property advice. We decided to sign up, and they have been a source of professional knowledge and information during this journey. We suggest you do the same or something similar. It is an excellent source of information, and you can call them at any time and ask questions on the phone. They also hold free seminars and have a monthly magazine full of advice and tips.

We were overwhelmed by the amount of companies at this exhibition. We advise if you do attend one of these exhibitions that you wear comfortable shoes, because you will be standing potentially for many hours, and walking around to all the different stalls, chatting to loads of people. Wear layers of clothes, as we have found that these venues can be temperamental, with the temperatures being from really warm and stuffy, to quite cool when the air conditioning comes on. Stay hydrated and drink lots of water; there are often water coolers at the site. It is easy to forget to drink water, and the consequence of this will leave you feeling even more tired at the end of the day.

Most of these types of events are free, and there are several seminars scattered throughout the day. In order to maximise your valuable time at this type of event, we suggest that you scour the seminar timetables to schedule your day around the seminars that you want to attend. Get to the seminars early, or book your seats to ensure you get a place.

As mentioned, it was here that we first met Kam, and during the seminar, Kam offered his book to someone who was willing to take action and get it. Jo stood up and grabbed the book out of his hand. Kam commented that successful people are the ones that are willing to get out of their seat, out of their comfort zone, and take action. We were delighted to have got Kam's book, and it is a fantastic read. So, check it out: *Boost Your Pension and Income from Property*. We liked the way that Kam was very real and approachable, even though he had a very large property portfolio, and is clearly very wealthy. After Kam's talk, this is where we signed up for the one-day seminar. Without the basic knowledge that we learnt from Kam, we would not be where we are today.

We have been to a variety of other free seminars about property, over the last 18 months. We have heard from high profile speakers, such as Rob Moore from Progressive Property. He is a self-made multi-millionaire, author and cofounder of the Progressive Group, including Progressive Education. He has a podcast called *The Disruptive Entrepreneur*, which we highly recommend.

We have also been to hear Kevin Green, from the Wealth Management Training Company. Kevin is a multi-business owner, and one of the UK's largest residential property landlords. He started life as a dairy milk farmer, and rose to his fortune by buying property. He also has a love for precious metals and gems, which he trades; and he has his very own mint, producing silver coins!

Watch out for free webinars about property investing. It's a fantastic way to learn about property from the comfort of your own home. As you can see, there is a lot of *free* information available. Content is not the problem. Bear in mind that further courses and seminars will be offered and sold to you. But remember, you need to spend money in order to make money. The good thing about webinars is that you can hear fantastic speakers from other countries, giving different perspectives. It doesn't matter where you invest in the world, property remains one of the best forms of investment, throughout the ages.

Networking Events are Crucial

"One of the most powerful networking practices is to provide an immediate value to a new connection. This means the moment you identify a way to help someone, take action."
– Lewis Howes

It's really important to be associated with the right group of people. Going out and about and meeting people who are likeminded to you is essential to develop your network. If you associate with people who are likeminded, then you'll have a better chance of meeting the right people who can help you make your business better. This can all come about by attending networking events.

Schedule in your diary the networking events that you intend to go to. This is what we did to start with. Make sure it is at least 1 a month—ideally more. Don't move it, don't delete it, and don't change it; keep it there in your diary, and go to it. There are several around where you live. You might just not know it yet. Type into Google, *property meeting in*, and then put your area. Find your nearest one, and attend.

We go to Premier Property Club networking events in London, and have been to various seminars, workshops, and online webinars. Premier Property holds several networking opportunities in and around London every month. There are always guest speakers, and an opportunity to mingle with new people and reunite with familiar faces. There is always an opportunity to ask the speakers questions in order to gain a deeper understanding of their specific field of expertise.

Another property network event that we attended was in Manchester, UK. We made contact with Fraser Macdonald. He runs a breakfast meetup group, once a month, at a local Manchester hotel. He is a highly experienced property investor with a large property portfolio, and he is well known throughout the UK. We signed up online and were delighted be able to secure a place, as we were aware that places were limited at this exclusive group. They like to keep the numbers low, and when we went there, there was no more than about 15 people. This was in order to give the attendees the opportunity to speak out during the intimate breakfast, and to talk about who they are, what they do, what they are looking for, and how they can help others.

After a full English breakfast, we were given the opportunity to speak to the group. We explained that we were new to property investing and, although we lived down in Hertfordshire, we have family connections in the Manchester area and have already purchased 4 properties in Greater Manchester. We had the chance to ask for recommendations for builders, and many people were forthcoming with information. Some of the attendees were offering joint venture opportunities. Others were offering private loans and property development opportunities, and we listened to stories of live ongoing projects locally. It was great to meet new people, exchange contact details, and to discover that these property investors were just like you and me. There was a range of experience—from us newbies to people who had been investing for 30+ years. We were delighted when Fraser suggested that we could join the WhatsApp group, which has proved extremely valuable. The WhatsApp group is used by investors who have attended the breakfast club. It is an active group, with people asking and exchanging information on a daily basis. At the meeting, we met a couple who were looking for joint venture investors who could contribute the money for their projects, while they would be hands on with any kind of development or refurbishment. We agreed to meet with them the following day to see two of their newly refurbished houses nearby, in order to see the quality of their work. They explained that they would be flipping (buy, refurbish, and sell) the two houses, and this is their usual model that they follow. It has been great to keep in contact with them on the WhatsApp group.

We also visited a group called Asana, which is based in Greater Manchester, UK. This was an evening group, where approximately 60 people attended. The host gave an overview of the current local property market position, and some of the new exciting projects and developments that they had coming up. Again, there was an opportunity to stand up and say who you are, what you do, and how you can help others. We sat at round tables of about 8 people per table. Although the group felt informal, there was a structure to the evening, and a guest speaker. He gave a talk on lease options, which is a bit too advanced for this book, but worth considering once you have been a landlord for a while.

It is great to have made so many connections within the area that we want to invest. These people have a wealth of knowledge that you can access, and they are often more than willing to help and advise, if you can be open and honest to the fact that you are new and open to learning. Every time we attend a networking event, we go with an open mind, and we always learn something new. We are able to build on the relationships that we are forming, building trust and friendship along the way. We often find that these events are uplifting. They rejuvenate our passion, and we get fired up again for the week ahead. It helps us to focus, and we gain practical knowledge that we can use for moving forward for future deals.

In the next chapter, we will show you how to become a successful property investor. We will teach you the strategies for success, practical advice about buying your first investment property, and the power of leverage.

Chapter 3

Strategies for Success

Research is imperative

"If we knew what it was we were doing,
it would not be called research, would it?"
– Albert Einstein

Gone are the days of having to go to your local library to do research. We remember being at school, studying for course work and looking up old newspaper articles on microfilm, which took hours! Now, everything is done on the Internet, and what a wonderful and beautiful thing it is! At your fingertips, you can get statistics, graphs, results, information, comparables, etc.

When you are looking for your buy-to-let (BTL) property, it is vital to get comparable properties and prices in the area. We tend to look at a ¼ mile radius (if there is enough to compare), and sold prices within the last couple of years. By comparing like for like on the type of property, you can get a good idea of the general sold prices in the area in which you are looking. By doing this, you are now much more informed to make a decision on the price.

Another good thing to find out about your BTL is how far the nearest supermarket is. Think to yourself... *Would this location be convenient?* By doing this, you will be thinking like your tenant, and asking the same questions that they will be thinking about when looking for a place to rent. *Are there good transport links?* By doing a quick search, you can find a whole host of train and bus times, plus the nearest major roads into or out of a town or city. It is a good idea to research what local infrastructure is in place now, considering shops, malls, cinemas, restaurants, leisure facilities, schools, universities, etc. You can also research future infrastructure, and look at local government plans to get an overall picture of the future of an area.

There may be a new train line planned that will be going close to your property. Is it too close? You will need to investigate further and decide. It might be fantastic news, as it might not impact your property in terms of sound and vibration, but it will be linking up an existing network, making your investment increase in price in the future. It is easy to take the information at face value... it's not ideal to have a train line running at the back of their house; however, on further investigation, it might be four roads away! By doing this research, you are painting yourself a large picture, and colouring in the detail. The more details you have, the clearer the picture becomes. This will help you to make a more informed choice about a particular street in an area. Generally, it is good to have family sized homes near high rated schools. You will need to research which schools are the best in your area. Certainly, in the UK, the closer you are within a catchment area to a particular school, the more likely you are of getting your child into that school.

We have found that researching comparable rental prices will help you to set a price for advertising your investment property. Don't just take the estate agent's word for it. Be prepared, and do your due diligence; this way will help you to come across more professional and more credible. Also, conduct some research on your managing agency. There are lots of different levels of service to managing your BTL. If you are close to your investment property, you may wish to be more hands-on, at least at the start, in order to understand the ins and outs of management. We, however, decided that not only were our properties too far away to manage, but that we didn't want to deal with the day-to-day issues of toilets not working, and lost keys. We would rather pay someone to manage this for us. The percentage charges and the fees differ greatly, so by doing your research, you can choose who is right for you. Bear in mind that this will not always be the cheapest. It is important that you really get on with the agent. Relationships are worth their weight in gold when it comes to management. You need to find someone who you can gel with. Have you ever wondered why it is called *research*, and not just *search*? That's because you have to go back and check and compare what you have initially searched!

In order to check that a potential property is a good investment, you will have to research and compare *like for like* properties, in regards to their rental income. Be sure to have the square meterage of each property that you are comparing in order to make your comparables stack up. When looking at an advertisement for property from an estate agent, have a look for the floor plan. This will give you a good insight before you go and visit the property, to see if the room layout is suitable and would meet the needs of a good rental property. We have seen some awful layouts of properties that do not flow. For example, the bedroom door not opening fully because the bed is in the way. Are the extensions or add-ons to the property legal? Were they under permitted development rights or was planning granted? Some properties may have had structural changes made, and planning was not requested or applied for through the local planning authority. It is possible that when applying for a mortgage in these sorts of circumstances that you will be required to obtain a lawful development certificate (LDC). Bear in mind that this can take a couple of months, and it costs the same as a planning application in the UK.

It's worth checking on which other estate agents are trying to sell the property that you are interested in. It's worth comparing sale offer prices, as this can also widely vary by sometimes £5K–£10K, or more. Having multiple agents selling one property could be an indication that the vendor is finding it difficult to sell. With your detective hat on, you will need to find out the reason why. Usually, you will also be able to see the sold price and date of sale. This will assist you with seeing if the asking price is reasonable. You will need to consider what, if any, refurbishments have taken place to the property since it was purchased by the current occupier or owner. Maybe the property has been extended, or a conservatory fitted. Also, if a full refurbishment has taken place, i.e. new boiler, central heating system, carpets, painting, and decoration, then this will reflect in a new higher asking price. So, don't just be put off because another house on the same street is for sale for a much lower price. All of these comparables need to be considered.

Additionally, it would be helpful to find out who the local authority is. Once this has been established, have a look at their policies. For example, if relevant, have a look at how the council is able to help with local school transport costs, what their recycling policy is, what the makeup of the various different political parties is, and if this will affect you or your tenants in some way. Maybe the tenants that you are trying to attract have particular religious needs. This may mean that certain prayer facilities will need to be local, and probably within walking distance. If these communities also have dietary requirements, can these be accommodated by local shops, or at least nearby?

Finding Your Goldmine Area

"Someone is sitting in the shade today because someone planted a tree a long time ago."
— **Warren Buffet**

Where are you going to look to buy property to invest in? Do you have a location in mind? Maybe it's the area that you live in, or maybe you have heard of a great hotspot, where all of the investors are going. Don't just jump into buying in an area because everyone else is. You still need to do your own due diligence, rather than going with the crowd. It is best to focus on an area that you are passionate about, or could become passionate about. Everybody's goldmine area is different, because everybody's needs and wants are different. This area needs to be somewhere that you are willing to invest a lot of time and a lot of money. You will need to decide whether property appreciation or cash flow is your main priority. Cash flow is the surplus money after all of your expenses have been taken into account from the income rental. Appreciation of a property is the increase in valuation of the property, which you can remortgage and take out the excess capital.

It might be that you are very young and can take full advantage of appreciation, as time is more likely to be on your side than someone in their retirement years. There are pros and cons for both. You will hear, in the property investing circles, that *cash flow is king*, and this is what we have decided to focus on. For us, cash flow is our main priority, and appreciation comes in second place. With this in mind, buying to hold and rent out is the property investor's perfect scenario. Why get rid of the *golden goose* when you get *golden eggs* every month? Your property investment becomes an asset—something that you can benefit from financially and then pass onto your children or loved ones when you die. We believe that buying single lets to rent is the best way for a property investor to start out. Only once you have been a landlord for some time, and have gained the knowledge and experience of property investing, should you look to other strategies and develop your portfolio.

Your goldmine area is a location where you can achieve purchases that are below market value (BMV), and which offer a yield of above 5% if in a major city, or above 7% outside a major city. The yield of a property is the amount of money that you can get in rental in proportion to the amount that you have invested into it. It has been said over and over to us that your goldmine area should be no more than about 30 minutes from your main residence. Although this is a great idea in principle, we found that because we are focusing on cash flow, and not on capital appreciation, the yields were too low within 30 minutes of our home. This is due to the house prices being substantially high down south. So we looked further afield to Manchester, UK, where the yields were twice as much! This was approximately 250 miles away from our home, and 4½ hours in the car. Jo has a connection with family up north. Jo's father grew up in north Manchester, and she has extended family living in the area. We felt it was a good place to buy property. It has been difficult at times being such a long way away, especially during refurbishments and keeping an eye on the building team. However, the benefit has been that we can take a short break and stay over in Manchester every 6 weeks or so, and enjoy the time away together, mixing business with pleasure. Ideally, a closer location would have been more preferable in order to reduce travel times and costs, but we are able to offset these expenses against income, for tax purposes. Your accountant will be able to give you more advice about this.

You need to find an area that ideally has the following: a good area will include close proximity to rail and bus links, or some kind of transport network; and access to local shops and supermarkets, prayer areas, gyms, and leisure facilities. Check with the local estate agents, compare your findings with let prices online, and find out how much a typical rental property is in the area. This will help you calculate the yield of the property. To calculate the gross yield, you need to multiply your monthly rental income by 12, and then divide that by your purchase price and other building costs. If you then multiply this by 100, you get the gross rental yield as a percentage.

Taking the time to do a drive around has proved very helpful. We could see the bad areas of a town that we wanted to avoid—the ones with mattresses left out on the pavement, rubbish not collected, and graffiti over local shop windows and walls. Equally, we discovered that the *posh* areas would not give good rental yield. We found that the happy medium in our area was where the people were of working class, with small family homes.

Speaking to an estate agent about the good and bad areas of your goldmine area will help you to identify the better streets, and the ones to stay clear of. Our mentor, Kam Dovedi, advised us to purchase three maps covering our goldmine area, and to approach three different estate agents. He said to get them to draw on our maps, the good and the bad areas, and once we had done all three, we could compare the results, which would give us a much clearer picture. We found this exercise to be very helpful. It clearly identified the better areas and helped us to focus on the streets that we should research to buy property in. This saved us a lot of time and energy, as we leveraged the estate agent's knowledge. We will talk about other people's time later on in this chapter. Now that you have an idea of where your goldmine area is, we will give you the second strategy to success, which is the simple buy-to-let strategy—and perfect for buying your very first investment.

BMV – Below Market Value

"To hell with circumstances; I create opportunities."
– Bruce Lee

When searching to buy a property, it's best to try and find something that is below market value (BMV). This will allow you to achieve greater profit margins and potentially a high yield. There are numerous companies out there that will offer you the opportunity to subscribe to their services. These may include sending you targeted emails and information. One of the problems with these organisations is that you have to pay a finding fee and reservation fee. The reservation fee may be around £1,000, but the finding fee may be a percentage of the value of the property, or a figure in the region of £4,000. This subscription to this organisation will send you numerous opportunities, which may not be in your target area and, therefore, will just add to and increase the amount of emails you get from the usual estate agents and other finding companies. Once a property is found by this below market value organisation, and you have paid your fee, and if for some reason you withdraw from the process, they may not return your fee. So, be aware. Personally, we would suggest that you don't go down this line; and some mortgage companies certainly frown upon making purchases that are from these organisations that are selling below market value properties.

Research is the best way of identifying properties that are below market value, and the usual websites—Rightmove, Zoopla, PrimeLocation, etc.—are ideal for you to be able to do comparisons. An option that you can take up on is to create some leaflets. These are very economical; for example, a full-colour leaflet, printed to A5 size, with 1000 copies, is in the region of around £40, or it can be less. You can decide on glossy or matt paper, or to print single or double sided. If you print single sided, you stand a 50/50 chance of your leaflet dropping on the mat upside down. We think it's a good idea to print double sided, so they can see either side of the leaflet, and it tells them straight away what you're offering. You would have already done your research as to the value of houses or flats in that particular area, and then you would look for a property in need of some love—a property where maybe the garden is not particularly cared for, or maybe the driveway needs some attention—and that's the sort of property that you would want to drop a leaflet to. We're not suggesting that you would just go for a house that is untidy or run down. It may be in quite good order and visually aesthetically pleasing. So, we wouldn't rule out the fact that just because a house is either in a poor condition or in good condition, that either of them are preferential. Both of them are potential opportunities, and it may be that the occupier is in a distressed state. By that, we mean that they are in need of selling, and that maybe they are in need of money fast. They might be going through other financial difficulties at work, or going through a divorce. Maybe they have children who are shortly going off to university, and they are in need of further funds.

Suddenly, this leaflet dropping through the door is the answer to all their problems. This can be a win-win situation, where you're helping them to get out of their misery or distressing situation, and it can work well for you too. It may be that you've identified a particular street or road or area, and you want to drop leaflets at all of the houses, but you decide that you haven't got the time to do this yourself. This is where leveraging your time is so important. It may be an opportunity for you to put an ad on one of those cards in the window of a newsagent, inviting interested parties to do a leaflet drop for you; this can be very economical, within the region of £8 or £10 for an hour. Of course, you need to do a little bit of due diligence with anyone you employ, because you don't want them just to dump all the leaflets in the local bin, and then have them say they have delivered 200 leaflets into 200 letter boxes. Clearly, if you can approach an owner of a property directly, this can be very lucrative for yourself and for them, as they won't have to pay estate agent fees. This can then allow them to reduce the overall selling price, allowing you to achieve a below market value price

If you take a look at sites like Rightmove or Zoopla, you can see the prices that a property has sold for. No one really knows whether the property prices are going to continue to go up or down at the moment. Prices are slowly, slowly evening out, and even slowing down in areas of London and the surrounding M25 areas.

The reason that you want to buy a property that's below market value is so that you can refurbish it, remortgage it, and get all of your money out of the deal, quickly. We suggest that you should try and be able to get all of your money out within two years. Work it out how much rental per month—if that's the path you're going down—and take away the costs of your expenses, i.e. your mortgage, insurance, and you should, within 2 years, get most of your money back. Don't forget that you will have to pay tax on your income. Some property education companies promote the ideal situation of getting all of your money out of the deal straight away. However, this is quite difficult to do, and you will spend a lot of time looking for this type of deal and may miss out on other great opportunities. So, the key here is research: you need to look at figures; you need to look at potential costs. Taking the time to do this essential part of searching for that ideal below market value property is the key to success in property investing.

BTL – Buy to Let

"Before anything else, preparation is the key to success."
– **Alexander Graham Bell**

Buy to let is the most simple and easiest way to make money from property. In fact, everyone that we have learnt from or been mentored by has said to focus on this first, and get good at it before moving onto any other type of property investing. It is a simple way of turning your cash into a fountain of never ending cash flow—your own personal ATM.

Buy to let, sometimes referred to as *buy to rent,* is where an investor buys a property and rents it out on a single tenancy—for example, to a family. A buy-to-let property could be a flat or a house. The idea here is that you buy a property that is undervalued, give it a light refurbishment, and then rent it out. You could refinance the property after 6 months to see if your refurbishment has given the price an uplift, but we think it is better to wait until your mortgage is up for renewal—say in a couple of years. This way, you will not have to pay for any early redemption charges, and it gives the property time to increase in value naturally. The last thing you want is to refinance 6 months later, pay out for another valuation, and get an early redemption, to find that it has only added a small amount of uplift to your property. It is better, in our view, to get the property rented as soon as possible, and to get it cash flowing for you!

Buying property is the only asset class in which you can ask the bank to lend you up to 80% of the entire value. Imagine going into your bank and asking to borrow £100K to invest in the stock market, or to buy precious artwork, or a vintage car. They would laugh at you and tell you to get lost, in so many words. However, if you are able to fund the other 20% or 25% as a deposit, and the other legal costs involved (for example, stamp duty, solicitor's fees, etc.), then the banks will be delighted to pass over their money to you. The history of the property market is where the banks get their faith. You can clearly see on charts and statistics that, over time, property prices always rise, making property a sound investment. When calculating the deal on a property, take into consideration void periods. Ask local letting agents in the area what the typical void period is. It might only be 5%, which is great; however, it may be a lot higher, meaning that there is not as much demand for the rentals as you may have thought at first. You will need to sit down and work out all the expenditure for the property, including a maintenance cost (depending on the condition of the property), compared to what you will be getting in. If you are getting in more money than you are spending on the property, then it is a positive cash flow. If, however, you have worked out the cost of the mortgage, voids, maintenance, etc., and you are spending more than you are getting in from the rental, then this is a negative cash flow, and you can discard this property off your list of potential purchases.

It is a good idea to set up an Excel spreadsheet in order to keep track of the properties that you are looking at. Be sure to include a column for each of the following:

- Address
- Price
- Square metre of the property
- When the property was first listed
- EPC rating
- Parking
- Garage
- Garden
- Which floor the property is on
- How many bedrooms

- Is there a buying chain
- How close to the train stations
- How close to the shops
- What is the overall condition of the property
- Leasehold or freehold
- Length of lease
- Who is the agent
- Viewing date and time
- Offer made and date
- Notes on the property

Visit www.phillipsrealestate.co.uk/book for a blank template to start you off; otherwise, you could keep track of your properties in any format you like. The purpose of tracking is to be able to easily see what you have discarded, and to be able to compare properties, to see which ones are the best for your circumstances.

The best type of properties are those that are classed as *chain free*. This means that the vendor does not need to find a property themselves; they can leave the property vacant, and the sale can progress swiftly. Be aware that properties that are not chain free can take a lot longer to go through the selling process. Not only do you need to consider the vendor's situation of the property that you are buying, but you will need to consider the next vendor situation down the chain. That person may or may not be chain free. The longer the chain of buyers, the longer it generally takes for everything to go through the process. As you can see, the more properties you have in the chain, then the more things there are to go wrong. Sometimes a property is offered with what is called a *sitting tenant*. First, ask yourself why the vendor is selling. It might be because he has had a terrible time with the tenant, and wants nothing more to do with them or the house!! Or it might be nothing to do with the tenant. Bear in mind that this will be an unsettling time for the tenant, especially if they have been in the property many years, and they consider it their home.

We have found that the more questions you ask, the better. Sometimes your questions will lead to other questions, and could open a can of worms. At least you can be better informed to make a judgement of which property to buy.

Leverage is a Game Changer

"You are either leveraging other people's time towards your vision or being leveraged by someone else working towards their goal."
– Rob Moore

This was a big eye opener for us. All your life you are taught to do things for yourself. You get taught that independence is the way forward. Even at school, you do your exams all on your own. When we discovered about leverage, our world changed. It suddenly freed us up to do more of the things that we actually enjoyed, and that we wanted to spend time doing. We looked at all of the things in our life that we do, and we figured out what we didn't enjoy. We chose to leverage out a cleaner, saving us four hours a week. We also decided to leverage our bookkeeping. We were spending far too much time looking at how to do the bookkeeping and how to record stuff properly. It was taking up lots of our time, and lots of our brain power—and we didn't even know if we were doing it right! By getting a bookkeeper, this freed us up from the challenges of having to record everything. It's not even that much money! Now we can focus on buying properties.

There are lots of different things you can leverage. You can also leverage knowledge. Learning all this new information helped us to get things right the first time. We also decided to leverage our time cooking, by eating out whenever we go to a networking event or a seminar day.

On average, most people have more than twice as much debt as savings. How long would it be before you were in financial difficulty?

On average, in the UK, it is after only 2 months.

Rich people know that by getting you to work harder and longer for money, it keeps you in a job. This allows them to leverage your time for them. So why not get other people to do work for you. If you have 20 people working for you a day, for 8 hours, then your day effectively can increase to 160 hrs. If you get 200 people to work for you, then your average day can be 1600 hours. Think what could be achieved with all that leveraged time. Poor people exchange their time for money. Rich people leverage other people's time.

Leveraging is not just about getting other people to do property-related tasks. In your personal life, if you get someone to cook for you, iron your clothes, clean your house, drive you to a meeting, mow the lawn, and do your garden, then you will have more time to do other tasks that will generate an income for you. You can use that time to generate 5, 10, or maybe 50 times or more, what you have just leveraged.

Work out what your average hourly rate from your income is. Then, if there is a task that costs less than your hourly rate, you can allocate that out to someone else to do. It is well worth doing a comprehensive diary, for a month, of what percentage of your time is actually spent on income generated tasks, and how many hours you put in to earn money. How much do you actually earn? Then, divide the income by the amount of hours. This will give you your income generated value. So, simply, if something is going to bring you in more per hour than your income generated value, then you will do this yourself (See Rob Moore's book, *Life Leverage*, for a more detailed explanation of IGTs). What this also identifies for you is if there is a task to carry out, and the hourly value is going to be less than your income generated value, then get someone else to do it. So, leverage it out.

So, to get rich, you need to surround yourself with other skilled people that can do IGTs for you. Remember, you are expendable. There is always someone else that can carry out a role that you have been doing. Try and get over the mindset that you are so unique, and that no one else can do the task as well as you. We actually do this already, if you think about it. If you were going to buy a property, you wouldn't negotiate your own mortgage; you might go to a broker or to a bank that has the experience and all the systems in place. If you were going to give contracts to a new tenant, you wouldn't write the contracts yourself; you would maybe utilise a property management company who has the tried and tested expertise in this field. Would you go to a prospective property you wish to purchase, and carry out your own survey? No, you couldn't. Would you paint, decorate, change the central heating system, change any double glazing windows, and fix a leaking roof? You might have a go at some of these tasks, but how long would it take you, and to what standards? You need professionals who have the experience to do these tasks efficiently and promptly.

Systems are Imperative

"I believe that if someone else can do something, then so can I."
– Darren Winters

We have been advised to systemise Phillips Real Estate Ltd over the last year or so during our property journey. There are all kinds of different ways you can streamline your business with different software packages and apps. The one we prefer is an app called BaseCamp. It is an all-singing, all-dancing way to track projects, schedule appointments and meetings, and message about specific projects, or to individuals, and much more. We came to use this particular system because our property partners were using it, and they wanted us to join their system so that they could communicate and streamline the projects we appraise for them. There were a few other systems we tried, and we particularly like Asana but settled with Basecamp, as:

1) We were already using it with Development Discovery, our partners;
2) It is super user friendly; and
3) It meets our needs.

Basecamp is a fantastic way to organise groups, teams, and projects. There is a *Docs* section within each project, to log all our documents associated with our BTL project (e.g., EPC, mortgage details, electrical survey, gas safety certificate, quotes, tenancy agreements, etc.). Once you have clicked into the *Docs* section, you can create new folders or new documents, or upload files from your computer.

We have found the following folders useful to have:

- Appraisals
- Reports and Searches
- Professional Team
- Management
- Planning
- Photos
- Market Information
- Finances
- Legal
- Refurbishment

By keeping all your documents, notes, reports, and files in a selection of folders, it makes it very easy for: 1) ease of reference; and 2) someone else to take over if necessary. This is where you can also load up your Excel spreadsheets that you are filling in for your viewings. If you use Google Drive or something similar, you will be able to update the document and have it as a *living document* that can be altered and changed as you go along. There is a *to-do* section within Basecamp, where you can create multiple lists of things that need doing. Here is where it is best to write out your check lists for a property. There is a facility to assign a particular task to an individual, and a specific date that it needs to be completed by. There is a handy tick box next to each task, and it is surprisingly satisfying to click *complete* once the *to-do* is finished. We suggest you don't create a specific project until you have viewed the property and are prepared to put in more effort and time in the research. It can get too messy having multiple projects open at one time, if you do not plan to pursue them. It is a great way to collate all your information in one place.

There is a section for scheduling. Here, you can put in all the appointments and meetings that you have booked in for a project. You have the flexibility to assign numerous people to an appointment, amend the time and date, and add notes; and you can even choose who to notify when the scheduled appointment is created. Not everyone in your project will need to know about a meeting! The thing we particularly liked about the scheduling section is that you can link it up with your mobile phone calendar, and it automatically gets updated with the appointment that you are creating in Basecamp. It means you will not only not miss appointments, but you do not have to duplicate your time by adding two entries—one for the Basecamp, and one for your phone.

There is a section for storing important emails that are linked to the project. It is really easy to use! You just copy and paste a link into a forwarding email, and it goes directly into your BTL project. This is great if you need to go back to a specific email within a project, rather than looking through all your emails and hunting for the one you need. It is not important to keep all the emails relating to a particular project. However, it is important that you stay on top of the filing; otherwise, you could come to the end of the week and have a ton of admin tasks to complete just to stay afloat! Once you get bigger with your business, and have multiple properties to look after, you could consider having a PA (personal assistant) to do these admin tasks.

There is a message board section that is handy for telling others, who are involved in the project, details or updates about a specific topic.

There is a header choice for each message (for example, FYI, announcement, ideas, or questions). There is also a more informal *campfire* messaging system, which lets you talk freely about the project, in a non-structured way, much like Facebook Messenger or Whatsapp. Pings are for private messages but can be to groups of people—not just one to one. It is so great to have a system that is completely cloud based, and can be accessed anywhere, at any time, with the use of a laptop, iPad, or mobile phone. Having everything under one roof that is associated with the project helps you to keep your systems tidy and accessible to others involved. It is a brilliant system that is functional and friendly, and keeps you, your colleagues, and partners up to date. It really helps us to feel in control and to stay connected with the projects, and with others in our team.

Gone are the days of huge filing cabinets and rows and rows of folders! Although we do suggest that some important documents be paper filed and stored for safekeeping. Whichever way you prefer to systemise, you need to find the best way that suits you. It is vital that you get your systems and checklists in place first. In this chapter, we have told you some absolute gems about leveraging and systems. Now, come with us into the next chapter as we explore together in more detail about buying your first investment property.

Chapter 4

Outlining the Process

Finding Your Power Team

*"Teamwork is the ability to work together toward a common vision.
It is the fuel that allows common people
to attain uncommon results."*
– Andrew Carnegie

Mortgage Broker – The job of a mortgage broker is to find the best possible mortgage for you and your circumstances. They have connections with lenders and can get mortgage deals that will not be available to you and me. The mortgage broker will charge a fee, and this cost will need to be factored into your calculations. When you choose a mortgage broker, be sure to ask if they can research the *whole of the market*. You need someone who can offer a wide selection of lenders and products. They will ask for proof of funds, passport verification, utility bills to confirm your residence, income statements, and details about all your other properties in your portfolio (if you have one). If fact, it can appear to be a bit of a grilling, but so long as you go through the list systematically, and make sure you hand everything over to them on time, then you will go through this process more smoothly. There seems to be a lot more *hoops* to jump through in order to get a mortgage since the stock market and property crash of 2007/8. Lenders have been more stringent with their cross checks, and are not keen on over leveraging a deal. In the UK, it is likely that you will get 75% loan to value, or maybe 80% at a push. I have heard of the *heyday* stories, from back in 2005/6, where banks and other lenders would hardly check details of the client, and then get offered 125% for the deal! They were even giving money to the client to refurbish the property! It is clear that that is unsustainable, but a lot of people were hurt during that time, and for others, they made their fortune. It is important that you feel that you connect with your broker. Do they answer phone calls and emails in a timely fashion? Do you feel that they are doing their best to push your mortgage through? You will find all kinds of referrals for brokers during property network meetings and seminars, but like a lot of these things, it will be trial and error.

Solicitor – Finding a good conveyancing solicitor who pushes your acquisitions swiftly through the process, who is hard working, loyal, and can guarantee detail and attention, is going to be a case of trial and error also. We have made the mistake of using a friend's friend as a solicitor before. They were rubbish! And it then became a bit awkward talking with the friend that initially recommended them. You may have someone in mind already that you have used to purchase your own home, but bear in mind that some lenders will require a large firm, and often one that is on their own panel. Make sure that the solicitor that you choose is good for the lender too.

Builders - Finding a good building team and handyman have been our biggest challenges so far. We were lucky, I guess, with our own renovation team for our current home. At the time, we were frustrated with the length of time our refurb was taking; however, now in hindsight, and having completed other refurbishment projects, we can see that they were actually very good. It is only through experience and kissing a few frogs that you can find the good ones.

Here are some tips for finding a great builder:

- Ask for recommendations from friends, family, and other investors.

- Read the reviews on sites such as trustatrader.com, mybuilder.com, and checkatrade.com. Here, you will be able to find comments regarding the experiences of people who have already worked with the builders. You will be able to find a credible builder with a good track record.
- Find out how long the builders have been trading. You will then have a large pool of people to speak to.
- Get quotes, and compare like for like. Make sure that you get estimates for the length of time it will take, as well as the price.
- Be wary of cold calling from a builder. Great builders tend to be booked up weeks in advance, and have little or no need for advertising.

Bookkeepers – Early on, we realised that we were not great at the bookkeeping side of the business. We decided to get a package called Xero, which is a fantastic accounting software package that is fairly easy to learn. Even so, we kept forgetting to put entries in, and accounts didn't reconcile. We were advised to get a bookkeeper, but the cost seemed too high in the UK. A friend recommended that we consider using a bookkeeper from abroad, someone that was highly qualified and knew how to use the Xero software. We tried a 6-week period with a qualified accountant from Philippines, and haven't looked back since. We pay him above average because this meets the minimum wages in the UK, and we didn't feel right paying any less than this. Even though it is a low amount of money to us here in the UK, it will have huge purchasing power in another country.

Property Management – Another member of your power team is the managing agency. From what we have seen and heard, there are a lot of horror stories when it comes to management. Remember to consider that those are the stories that tend to get the attention and headlines, and not to judge a book by its cover, and that you should dig deeper. You don't tend to hear the stories of a management agency that was brilliant, handling everything and having nothing going wrong. It's not news! But this is exactly the sort of agency you want. It is vital that they don't choose just anyone to move into your property, but to find people that are going to be considerate and easy to get along with, and who will hopefully be living in your property a long time. Remember that there will be costs for finding the tenants, so the less often they leave, the less times you will have to pay to find someone new. It is important to feel that you can easily communicate with your letting agency, and talk about issues and problems as they arise.

Accountant – When it comes to accountancy, you will need to find a firm that deals specifically with property accountancy. There are so many different types of accountants, and having someone who knows specific property tax laws is vital. You need to find an accountant who keeps up to date with tax law legislation so that they can optimise your tax savings. You will find that you get referrals of accountants from property networking groups, and if you have a mentor, you can ask him or her who they use.

The people that you are choosing will form what we like to call your *power team*. This team of people will hopefully be with you through thick and thin in your property journey. It is important to choose wisely, and to make sure the team are all working in harmony together. We like to, as much as possible, pay the power team peeps on time, and with a thankful heart. If it weren't for them, then the whole thing could come to a grinding halt.

Good Relationships With Estate Agents

"Great things in business are never done by one person. They are done by a team of people."
– Steve Jobs

Going to estate agents and becoming a familiar face is a must. The sooner they know that you're serious, what you're looking for, how much you are looking to spend, and the exact area you want to purchase in, they will greatly assist. There are 4 types of estate agents. Firstly, there are national corporate agencies. This type of agency tends to have a hierarchy, whereby the employees are unable to purchase the deals that come up themselves. Next, are the regional chains. Just have a look about your area and see what names are on the *for sale* boards outside. This type of agency tends to be more flexible when dealing with investors. Next are the independent agencies. These guys tend to be the friendliest; however, they often get the deals for themselves before they go to market. Lastly, there are the letting agencies who think they are sales agents, when, in fact, the processes of selling a house is a completely different ball game from lettings. You may find deals come through them, but just be careful, as always, to do your due diligence.

Kam Dovedi, from Premier Property, talks about the different profiles of an estate agent.

Kam runs a 3-day workshop that we would highly recommend, which expands on these profiles. Once you know them, it really is easy to spot. There are those employees who are only there to do the bare minimum, and who will only help you if they have to. There are those that are confident, yet will screw you over to get the deal done. Then there are those people who are brilliant, who will work with you, and for you. They tend to be smart looking; they give the correct information; they are keen to help, and are bright- eyed and bushy-tailed. Another helpful type of estate agent is the one that has been there for years. We are talking like 20 years plus. They know how things are run; they keep a tight ship; they know what they are doing, and are excellent at negotiation. Then there are the managers. It is not best to approach these guys to start with, until you have bought one property. Once you have made that connection, they will be more than happy to help you after seeing that you are genuine and real about property investing. When you are more established, they will put you on a short list and contact you first thing—sometimes before the property goes onto the market on the usual property websites.

This can be a fantastic opportunity for you to have a first refusal, and for them to receive their quota and their percentage. There tends to be a fear amongst new investors about speaking to estate agents. It is easy to get yourself wound up, sweaty- palmed, and not come across well. It might be a good idea to practice with a friend by doing a role play, and maybe write out a short script of exactly what you want to say so that you become familiar with what you want to ask and say. You can also practice in front of a mirror and/or record yourself via your phone.

Estate agents have a wealth of knowledge that you can glean from: they know the local area property market prices; which streets are good, and which are not; and they will have dealt with local councils and can give you a heads up about what they are like to deal with. All of this knowledge is free by just speaking to them and building a relationship. Choose the right estate agent, and they will open up to you and tell you anything that you want to know about property in that area. Once you have identified your *goldmine area,* they can advise you on the best deals. It's all too easy to sit at home in front of your computer, on Rightmove or other estate agent portals, but there is nothing like speaking to someone and making a personal, face-to-face connection.

When you first walk into their office, decide who you want to have that connection with, and approach them and ask to register your details. We suggest that you dress smartly. Try and understand things from the estate agent's point of view. They may have had 10 other investors in that morning, all saying that they have lots of money for cash deals. Just be yourself, and remember to be flexible when arranging viewings. Once you have established this good relationship with your first contact, you will soon be on your way to becoming known in the whole office and, subsequently, your area. Try to remember that the estate agent is there because that is their job. They do it in order to get a commission and to get paid every month. They may not tell you about the planning application in the street that will devalue your property, or the potential subsidence or Japanese knotweed problem. Their intention is not to be kind but to sell the property and get their percentage. Be aware that there is a high turnover of staff within estate agencies. So be prepared to start a new relationship with an agent every 12–18 months.

There is nothing worse than appearing to bribe an estate agent by offering a small brown envelope with money in it. This will alienate you and blacklist you, and they won't want to work with you. This is not from personal experience, but we have been strongly advised to avoid this type of behaviour. When you buy a property from an estate agent, you do not pay any fees as the buyer. It is the vendor (seller) who has to pay an agreed percentage to the estate agent on completion of the deal. One idea to sway a vendor to sell to you, if there is multiple interest, is to offer to pay some or all of the estate agent fees. Make sure that you do your calculations in order to ensure that this remains a good deal. There is nothing wrong with giving a box of chocolates or a bunch of flowers to your estate agent once you have completed on your property. In fact, this is a great way of being thankful and being remembered. This can only be to your advantage, as you will remain within the forefront of their mind when a property of your criteria next comes onto the market.

Visiting the Property

"Look for 3 things in a person: intelligence, energy, and integrity. If they don't have the last one, don't even bother with the first two."
– Warren Buffet

Try to arrive 15 minutes before your scheduled appointment viewing time, and take a slow drive around the area. Make a note of nearby bus stops, local supermarkets, convenience stores, schools, nurseries, and fast routes into main towns or cities. See if the area looks well kept. Avoid areas that are grotty and are unkempt and use your sixth sense and intuition to judge the area. If you don't like it, then it is likely that your tenants won't like it either. Park near to the property, and just take a moment to take in the feel of the street. Open your car window and listen. If you do end up liking the property, then try to go back for a second viewing at different times of the day, and a different day of the week, to see if this changes your mind or influences you either way.

Take pictures of the outside of the venue, starting from the roof down. Note the condition of the roof tiles, and make any notes of any concerns to price up later. For example, note the condition of the gutters, woodwork, windows, and paintwork. Will the fencing need to be replaced sometime soon? Is the driveway in need of repair? Make sure that you arrive at the correct appointment time, and that you don't leave them waiting. Be personable and friendly, and remember to smile. It is better to go in with a small notebook to make notes as you walk around, rather than a clipboard. Some people will prefer to take notes/voice notes on their phone. We suggest that you take photos to document the property, because it's easy to forget what it looks like, especially if you're seeing a number of properties during the week. But make sure you get permission before you start snapping away.

Remember, at this stage, you may not know why the vendor is selling. It could be that they are going through a very difficult time. Once you go through the front door, take a note of its condition. Take a look around, and make notes using the following useful checklist, if viewing a typical, 3-bedroom house:

Downstairs:

- Radiators
- Painting and woodwork
- Flooring and carpets
- Light switches and sockets
- Light fixtures and fittings

- Internal doors and handles
- Fireplace
- Gas and electric meter
- Cracks in the ceiling or walls
- Dampness
- Kitchen condition (i.e. units)
- Work surface
- Electrical appliances (i.e. washing machine, dishwasher, oven, hob, extractor fan)

Sometimes the boiler isn't where you expect it. It can be under the stairs, in a kitchen cupboard, in the loft, in a bedroom, or even outside! Take a photo of the boiler, and find out how old it is, as well as when it was last serviced.

Step outside and have a look at the garden, and note the following:

- Roof (Check that it is sound.)
- Pipes
- Gutters
- Chimney
- Windows
- Brickwork (Check for any cracks.)
- Trees (If close to the property, they could cause a problem with the foundations.)
- Walls and fences
- Garden condition

Go upstairs now, and visit all bedrooms, looking at the general condition. Note the following:

- Wardrobes
- Windows
- Walls
- Ceilings

- Woodwork
- Fixtures and fittings
- Flooring and carpets
- Paintwork
- Radiators
- Loft and insulation (if applicable)

Take a look at the bathroom:

- Bath
- Taps and shower
- Toilet
- Flooring
- Tiles
- Windows
- Storage
- Extractor fan

When viewing a potential purchase, be mindful of the fact that you are visiting their home, whether it be a rental or owner occupied. So don't go in there explaining how you are going to completely redecorate, knock walls down, build extensions, etc., in front of the owner. Be polite and ask as many questions as you can. Here are some questions we suggest that you ask the vendor:

- Why are you selling?
- Have you tried to rent the property?
- Is the transaction chain free? (i.e. they don't need to find somewhere else to live before selling)
- Have you had any major repairs, or any major problems with the property?
- Is it leasehold or freehold? If leasehold, how much time is left on the lease?
- What are the typical gas, electric, water, and council charges per month?

- What are the neighbours like?
- Is there a mortgage on the property? (This is a little cheeky, but it can give you an insight into whether there may be some leeway with the price.)
- When were the electrics last upgraded?

Once you have viewed and left the property, you will have a good idea, and a gut feeling, whether you like it or not. It is only when you go back and crunch the numbers, including the refurbishment and redecoration costs required, that you will be able to put forward your offer.

Buying Your First Property

"If you spend too much time thinking about a thing, you'll never get it done."
– Bruce Lee

1) Mortgage Broker

The first port of call is to speak to your mortgage broker. They can assist you to find out exactly how much money you will have available for purchasing your investment property. This process can take a few weeks because there is a lot of documentation that the mortgage broker will initially need from you. You will need to get a decision in principle (DIP) from your broker, so that you know where you stand and what you can afford.

2) Viewing the property

At this stage, you find out exactly what needs to be done in order to bring the property into a lettable standard. It is here that you calculate all the potential additional costs that you could incur with the property. Be mindful to leave a contingency of about 20% to cover any unforeseeable costs.

3) Agree on a sale

There are plenty of other ways to find your property; for example, through family or friends. This is a great way to buy, as it cuts out a middle man, and ultimately can save you money. Finding deals through property networking groups, or on line, can also be advantageous, and sometimes another property investor could be looking to sell their whole, or part of their, portfolio. There are always good deals to be snapped up at auction, although we don't recommend this purchase option at the beginning, for your first property purchase—there is a lot more you need to know before the hammer goes down. Once you have done your calculations, and you are sure that the property will be good cash flow, you can make an offer of a price and negotiate the sale through the estate agent.

4) Mortgage application

At this point, a full application is made to a lender, in order to buy your specific property. There are sometimes costs at this stage—a broker fee.

5) Survey the property

This can take from a week up to a few weeks, depending on your lender. They need to organise, with the estate agent, access to the property, in order to complete their property survey. You will then get a report which you *must read* very carefully to avoid surprises down the line. This report will give a valuation of the property and how much the lender is prepared to lend you for a mortgage. You can decide then whether it's in your financial interest to purchase the property.

6) Instructing a solicitor

At this stage, it is prudent to have had a phone call with your solicitor, to ask them to send a solicitor's pack to you, ready for instruction. By this time, you will have completed the filling out of the pack and returned it to your solicitor. Therefore, this stage is easy, as it is either a phone call or an email instruction for them to go ahead and commence the various searches. The solicitor firm will generally ask for some money up front at this stage. The searches can take a couple of weeks—be sure to read the reports thoroughly. All kinds of things can be found on the searches; for example, the property could be in a flood risk area. There could be planning permission nearby for a new development, like a new shopping centre or motorway. Therefore, being forewarned is being forearmed.

7) Contracts signed and exchanged

It can take a number of weeks for all of the paperwork to be completed, and for all of the T's to be crossed and all of the I's to be dotted. Once your solicitor has exchanged the contracts, then the sale is legally binding (in the UK). Be sure to have prearranged your building insurance so that it commences the day you exchange contracts.

8) Completion

The day of completion is a day for celebration. Once all of the funds have been transferred by your solicitor to the vendor's solicitor, completion will have taken place, and the property is yours. This normally occurs around 12 noon, and tends not to happen on a Friday, because if for some reason there is a difficulty in the funds being telegraphically transferred, then you would have to wait until Monday for this to go through. You finally hold the keys to your first investment property. Normally, the keys will be left with the estate agent that the vendor has used.

9) Refurbishing your property

Ideally, you will have lined up your builders in advance so that they can commence works as soon as completion has taken place. The longer they take to start, the longer it will be before you see a return on your investment (ROI). Make sure that the builder has a copy of the key(s); otherwise, you will have to open and close up the property each day, and this will use up your time.

10) Letting the property

We would always advise using a letting agency to secure a tenant for you, and to manage the rental of the property on an ongoing basis. It is your letting agent's duty to compile a full inventory. This is a list of all the contents of the property, so that there is no dispute with a tenant when they leave (hopefully not for 50 years). The longer the tenant stays, and pays regularly and looks after your property, the better. Once the property is let, the money will effortlessly roll in. You will be required to have gas and electric safety certificates, and EPC (Energy Performance Certificate), given to your tenant prior to them moving in. Make sure that your tenant signs that they have received these documents; otherwise, you may have difficulties down the line.

Building Trust With Builders

"I know of no single formula for success. But over the years I have observed that some attributes of leadership are universal and are often about finding ways of encouraging people to combine their efforts, their talents, their insights, their enthusiasm and their inspiration to work together."
– Queen Elizabeth II

As previously mentioned, one of the most essential components of your power team is your builder. Be sure to find a builder who is not a one-man band, and who has access to various tradesmen that are required to complete your project. These can include joiners, bricklayers, roofers, tilers, electricians, and painters. A good builder is usually not readily available, and gets booked up in advance. Be prepared to wait if you want a specific company to complete your project. All of your payments to your builder need to be recorded, and the best way to do this is to pay via a bank transfer (i.e. BACS). This way, if there is any discrepancy, then you can easily check out the actual payments. So, we would suggest, from the start, when you first meet your prospective builder, that you, in the best possible way, make it clear to him what your ground rules are going to be; and if there is going to be an issue with this, you really should consider choosing someone else to assist you on your project. This can be very frustrating, especially if you are favouring this company. It is certainly about forming a good relationship with your builder and their team.

Always go and stick with your gut instinct, which generally will be right. Make sure that you have their address, mobile and landline numbers, and email details. We have found that most builders don't have their own website as, generally, word of mouth is the way that builders get their next job. I'd also be cautious of a builder that turns up to a site visit dressed up smartly. We like to feel that the main guy that you will be dealing with will be on site all or most of the time, getting his hands dirty and getting into the project. When you visit a completed project of your prospective builder, take a note with regard to the finer detail. For example, is there paint over the electrical switches, and has there been care and attention to the paintwork? Has any of the door furniture been painted over? Is the kitchen square, and are the ceramic tiles flat, with even grouting?

Doors sometimes require replacement, so have a look at the way the hinges have been put on. Sometimes a builder with poor joining/ carpentry experience will need to put on and take off hinges a number of times, and this indication may show poor competence. Look at how the door is painted around the hinge, or even over the hinges. This is not a good sign. This shows a lack of care and attention, and this is an indicator of how your project will be completed. The finishing touches to a property can really make or break the difference of a higher quality finish. Make sure that all the doors open easily, and that a consideration has been made to allow for carpets. It is always a good idea to clarify any of your requirements in writing. Email is definitely the best way to go forward. It allows you to easily search for a conversation; whereas using texts and WhatsApp-like applications don't. We also found that getting the builder to send photos of the progress was a good way to manage them. This is also useful to see evidence of their workmanship, and these photos can also be used if you have a website.

If things do go wrong, make sure that you keep the lines of communication open. Don't be defensive—be assertive, and clearly state what you are trying to achieve and how you need the problem rectified. In order to give the builder an incentive to finish your project in a timely fashion, have discussions regarding future work; for example, your next project. Don't rely on one builder to do all of your projects. Have a minimum of 2, so that you can rotate the works, and if you are let down, then you have a backup team.

It is good practice to have at least a 15–20% contingency. This means that as your project continues, in the event of an issue arising, you won't get caught with not having sufficient funds available to deal with this problem; for example, a leaky roof needing repair, or a front door requiring replacement. Ideally, when your builder does their initial site survey and breakdown of all costs, you will have a heads up on any potential issue or things that you may not have noticed. Any good builder will know that he will need to ensure that the property is completely watertight—so, working from the top down and then dealing with other issues as they appear.

Letting the Property & Management

"You can do what I cannot do. I can do what you cannot do. Together we can do great things."
– Mother Teresa

Whilst your builder is on site, it is a good opportunity for you to find the letting agency that is right for you. You need to decide whether or not you want to take on the management of the property yourself, or whether you are prepared to pay for services of an experienced professional. What is more important to you? Do you want to be hands on and learn the ropes of being an on-call landlord yourself, or would you prefer not to be involved at all? We have decided on the latter. Not only are we miles away from our investment properties, we don't want to have the responsibility and hassle of sourcing tenants, dealing with ongoing maintenance, and collecting rent. There is no right or wrong answer here, but consider how valuable your time is, and if it could be better spent elsewhere.

By looking at comparables of letting agent fees, and speaking to letting agents in the area, you will get a feel for who to work with. Remember, this investment is for the long term and, therefore, you will need to be sure that the letting agency you choose is right for you. Personalities are very important here. Feeling totally at ease that your point of contact is someone you can trust and get along with, is crucial. Here is a list of some considerations when choosing your management company:

- What length of time have the directors and employees been working as an agency?
- How many properties are they currently managing?
- How do they vet their tenants?
- What are their fees, and are there any extra fees?
- How many tenants have they had to evict over the last few years?
- Are they a member of any professional bodies?
- Where do you advertise the availability of the property (i.e. which media platforms)?

Do not be worried about asking for further information about their property journey. Try to make it informal, and add it in during a conversation, rather than going into the office with a list of questions. Ask about references of tenants and the general length of time that their tenants stay in the properties that they manage. Remember that property investing is a team sport, and management is a big part of the overall game. Who will be the tenant's first point of contact? Is that person personable, approachable, and firm; and how quickly do they fix problems that come up? If they have had a large number of evictions, then maybe they are not the agency for you, as they may seem not to have a robust system in place for choosing the right tenant. The fee that management companies charge can be variable, depending on the agency and type of letting. We have found, typically, that agencies can charge anything from 8–12%, or higher. We negotiated 8% for our buy-to-let properties, as we mentioned that we were looking to own over 200 properties, and that we would be happy for this particular company to manage all of our properties. This *carrot* assisted in getting a reasonable rate. The management of HMOs is much more time consuming and problematic, so expect a higher management fee if this is your direction.

When a new tenant moves in to your property, they will also take on the responsibility of making contact with the local authority, and all the utility companies, to ensure that your name is taken off the bills. The new tenant then continues to make the payments. Make sure that you cancel any direct debits you may have set up. Just for peace of mind, knowing that the gas meter and electric meter have been read and the numbers recorded, makes sure that you only pay what you are due to pay, up to the point that the new tenant moved in.

If you think these tips have been useful, just wait until you get to the next chapter, where we can get down to the nuts and bolts, and give you even more tricks and tips of where and what to buy.

Chapter 5

Where and What to Buy

The Fundamental With Appraisals

"It always seems impossible until it's done."
– Nelson Mandela

Having an appraisal is a way of collating all the information about a property, BEFORE you decide to purchase it. It is important that all the sections in the appraisal be filled in, so that you can make a sound judgement on whether to make an offer, or how much to offer, on your BTL property. You can download an appraisal form from our website, or feel free to create your own that suits you. Please visit our website, at www.phillipsrealestate.co.uk/book, now.

An appraisal document can be created on Google Drive, enabling it to become a *living document* that you can alter and update as your project moves forward. We have found that the following sections need to be included in the document:

- Address of the property
- Asking price, want, like and acceptable price
- Overview of the deal, including stamp duty, yield, strategy, and refurbishment costs
- General comments
- Infrastructure
- Private and public future investments

- Maps with distances
- Local amenities
- Details of the local authority and a local plan
- Tenant market research
- Comparable sold prices
- Estate agent details
- Floor plans
- Renovation detailed costings
- Financial appraisal
- Local letting agency details

By having a document ready to fill in, it will ensure that you don't miss a vital section of the analysis. It may seem daunting at first, but once you have done it a few times, you will soon get the idea of how to appraise an investment property. You will be surprised at how much information you already have, just by doing some of the basic research. It is here that you will be able to see if the property is worth making an offer on. When looking at the infrastructure in an area, consider schools, universities, supermarkets, leisure and sports facilities, cinemas, shopping centres, train stations, and nurseries. Also consider your target audience. Have a look at the local authority website to see what plans are in place for the future. Local authorities are obliged to have a local plan that they are putting into place to improve the area for its residents. There might be details of an upcoming renovation of an old and unloved shopping mall or retail park. This kind of information could give you an edge when it comes to making an investment in the area. Most people looking to buy a house or a flat do not go into this much depth when finding themselves a home. By being fully aware of the future plans of a town or village, you will be able to see the deals that others might not see. By looking on Google Maps, you will be able to put in the directions from the investment property to a particular place of importance. Short distances to supermarkets and schools are essential. Train station distances are also especially important to tenants, and they often don't want to walk much more than about 10 minutes to get to a station. We like to take a screenshot of the journey, from Google Maps, and compare walking, cycling, and bus times.

Be sure to note all the costs, and to put in a contingency for the unknowns that may spring up once the works are underway. It is important to compare the rental prices with as many rental prices of a similar property to yours. There would be no point just selecting 5 properties to compare. Depending on which ones you choose, it could give you a very different answer. It takes a bit of time and a calculator, but we think it is a task well worth doing to get a really good indication of what your property is likely to rent for.

Floor plans are not something that every agent provides. Some do; some don't. As an agency, it is an additional expense to have a floor plan created by an expert and, therefore, you will find that some don't even bother. We used to find this annoying at first, and because we couldn't see a floor plan, we thought, *"If you can't be bothered to create a floor plan for us, then why should we spend time looking at this offer?"* When we said this to our mentor, Kam Dovedi, from Premier Property, he said that we were missing a trick! He turned the situation completely on its head, saying, *"Well, if everyone thinks like that, then there is less competition for you! Why not measure it yourself? It won't take long."* We understand that it is an effort to measure; however, now, with these amazing electronic mobile measuring kits, you can plan out a flat in no time. Even if it is a rough one, it is better than nothing! At least you have something to compare it to when your competition dismisses it. There is a great website, called Roomsketcher, which offers a free tool in order for you to plot your rooms. The appraisal will allow you to put all the financial details of the project together. This is a crucial part of the overall appraisal, and shows a clear indication if this property will be a successful investment or not. We tend to do a screenshot of the excel spreadsheet, and insert it into the appraisal document. Once you have all of the information together you will be able to make a final assessment to see if the deal will work. It is a good idea to have 3 prices in mind. Firstly what you would want to pay for the property, another that would be OK and the last is your bottom line for making the deal work. Be sure that you don't go above this price. Now you are ready to make your offer.

How to Find The Best Property

"Thoughts become things. If you see it in your mind,
you will hold it in your hand."
– Bob Proctor

Once you have decided on your goldmine area, there are a number of different aspects to consider. One of the best ways to purchase a property is to find something that looks distressed, or in *need of love*. It could be that the garden is overgrown, or the windows and doors have paint peeling off them. These are opportunities for the savvy investor, as it will most likely pull the price down and put off a lot of buyers.

Try to look at the house you are buying, from your tenant's point of view. Off street parking, easy walking distance to local shops and amenities, as well as being a low-crime area with good street lighting, is always advantageous. Make sure that the house has a good mobile phone signal, and an ideally fast broadband or fibre optics connection. Things to watch out for are large pylons, cemeteries, poor lit areas, small room sizes, and poor flow of water. Be aware of very large trees nearby, as their roots can be invasive to the foundations of the property, and can cause problems in the future. There is a plant, called Japanese knotweed, which is extremely aggressive and can grow up to 4 inches a day in summer months. It can even grow through concrete. Unless you know what you are doing with this plant, then it should not be touched; and we suggest you avoid buying the property, as it can become very expensive to eradicate. See the Royal Horticultural Society website for more information: www.rhs.org.uk/advice.

Auctions may be a great source of getting a property for a good price. However, we would not advise that you go down this pathway at this stage, as it can really be a money pit; and if you don't know what you are buying, you could run into a host of problems. We attended an auction in Manchester, UK, in order to experience what it was like. We would recommend that you visit an auction just to have this experience, and to gain some understanding for the future. In the room, there were about 200 people who were bidding on properties ranging from £30K–£3 million-plus. It was very exciting watching how fast the bids were made, considering the incremental jumps in the money. We sat on our hands, not wanting to scratch our nose or stretch, in case we accidentally made a bid.

At the early stages of finding your first property, we would recommend you stick to estate agents. See Chapter 4 for our thoughts and comments.

Let your friends and family know that you are a property investor. Spreading the word may get you an introduction to someone who is looking to sell but is maybe unsure, and after a conversation, you may establish a relationship whereby you can avoid the vendor having to pay 1%+ agent fee. This can be a savings of a lot of money, depending on the final agreed price.

Leafleting can be a very smart way of buying a property that is off market. Your leaflet needs to be clear, concise, and attractive to the homeowner. It could say the following:

"Would you be interested in selling your property?"

There could be prompts on the leaflet: *Are you going through a divorce? Are you looking to downsize?* It just might be that your leaflet falling onto their doormat is precisely what they needed at that time. You could produce a small card that is handwritten, and then, with the use of highlighters, you can draw attention to the opportunity. The leaflet will need to have:

- Your details (i.e. your name)
- Contact telephone number
- Email address

We were told by our mentor that it is always best to buy the worst property but on the best street. Make sure, though, that you can buy it at the right price and add value to it. If you are looking to build a large portfolio, then the above strategy is for you, and will keep your money working for you. However, if you are looking for only 1 or 2 properties to invest in, then you might not be too concerned in getting all of your money out immediately. You could look for a property that is in good condition and has a sitting tenant. With a managing agent to assist, you can be completely hands off, and just enjoy the monthly passive income.

Start With Buy to Let

"For me, the winning strategy in any start-up business is to 'think big but start small.'"
– Carmen Busquets

Everybody that has advised us has told us to start off simple. Within property, a BTL (Buy to Let) is the simplest type of property investment out there. They can give consistent returns for the least stress or headaches! It might be tempting to look at other projects and other property investment, but the good old BTL will indeed help you to understand the fundamentals, without too much of the risk to start with!

There are all kinds of different investments out there to look at in the future. You could purchase a block of flats rather than just one; you could buy one property and title split it into two properties. You could buy commercial properties or businesses, or buy to lease to businesses. You could buy land and develop commercial properties or residential properties from scratch. You could buy commercial properties and convert them into residential use. You could buy an existing HMO, or commercial to HMO development. You could Joint Venture with another person or a business. You could become a hands-off investor. You could own a hotel, a campsite, or yoots! You could do sourcing for other investors! The possibilities are endless, but hands down, nothing beats a good old fashioned BTL to start with.

It is well worth the wait, the patience, and the experience of a light refurbishment, and being a landlord or lady, without all the additional complications that these other property deals can bring. We suggest that you focus on BTL to start with, and once you have done a few and got enough confidence to know what you are doing, and gain the contacts and networks, only then go onto something else that might take your fancy. It is all too easy to be offered a deal that seems like a great profit or a solid investment opportunity, but remember not to run before you can walk. You can thank us later!

What sort of a property is a buy to let? This can be a flat or a house. It can be 1, 2, or 3+ bedrooms. It can be a terraced, detached, or semi-detached property that is either leasehold or freehold. The idea is that you purchase this property, get a mortgage on it, and then rent it out to tenants, and you charge them a rent. This rent covers the mortgage and any other overheads, and you make a profit. All the utilities and service charges, including any government taxes, are paid for by the tenants—you will just be responsible for the building insurance.

What is a buy-to-let mortgage? In order to buy your investment, you need a buy-to-let mortgage. If you have the money, you could buy it outright; however, you miss a trick on leveraging the bank's money. This sort of mortgage is good debt. A buy-to-let mortgage is a loan from a bank, which you pay back over a number of years. The rates available are usually higher than a standard residential mortgage, and you will need a larger deposit too. There are rates that offer 85% loan to value, but be cautious of stretching too far with your finances; options of 75% loan to value will have more reasonable rates. There are risks involved, and this needs to be mentioned. If your property, for some reason, is left unoccupied, there may be a chance that you will be unable to keep up your monthly mortgage repayments. This could lead the bank to repossess your property, so voids need to be considered. A void is a period of time that the property is unoccupied and you are not receiving any income. The other risk to also mention here is if there is a substantial cost required to repair something major. There is a risk if you do not have a sinking fund, or monies set aside— then you could be in major difficulties. These matters need to be considered and calculated into your purchase. Finally, if there is a drop in housing prices in your area, then your property may be of less value than you paid for it; and therefore, you drop into negative equity.

When interest rates go up, typically, your mortgage rate will go up, and so will your   monthly repayments. This may force you to need to increase your monthly rental, and tenants may not be happy with this. To keep your monthly mortgage payments low, you may consider an interest-only mortgage. This means that however long the period of the loan is from the bank, you will only be paying off, monthly, the interest on the loan amount, and at the end of the term of the mortgage, you will still have the same amount of capital debt to repay. This may seem counterintuitive; however, due to inflation, a £60,000 loan will now be worth a lot less in 20 years' time.

Also consider though, if you are buying a property with tenants in situ, then it can be problematic and disruptive to the tenant, if you need to do any major refurbishments in order to update tired decoration, or need to replace the kitchen or bathroom.

When we received our first rental money for our first buy to let, it was a wonderful feeling. We were delighted, and went out and celebrated. It is important to celebrate these seemingly small victories. We were finally able to officially say that we were landlords and property investors.

Light Refurbs Only

"Everything that is coming into your life you are attracting into your life, it's what you're thinking
– ***Bob Proctor***

The most important thing to remember is that this property you have purchased is an investment property. You are not going to be living there and, therefore, your personal tastes should not apply. You will need to consider your tenant profile, and deliver good quality properties that will encourage your tenants to stay in situ for a long time. We have found that doing structural changes takes a lot of time and extra money, and doesn't always give you the return on investment that you had hoped for. There may also be a requirement to obtain consent from the local authority regarding building regulations. If you are doing structural changes, this can delay the finish schedule, and will delay the arrival of your first monthly rental income. It is best to avoid structural changes and stick to light refurbishments only, or at least until you have got a few BTL properties under your belt!

By refurbishing a property, you are creating value by making a tired property look uplifted or new again. This is easily achieved by painting the walls, recarpeting, putting in a new fireplace, etc. If you make big structural changes, like moving a staircase or adding an extension, then this could eat into your overall profits and defeat the purpose of the entire investment! All the calculations for the refurbishment need to be done BEFORE you make the purchase. By systematically going through the property and adding up what each job is going to cost, you will come out with a full appraisal on the cost of the whole refurbishment. By having this information, you can make an offer accordingly, or walk away and not touch the property! Larger contractors are usually not interested in small refurbishment projects. They will have their eyes on bigger projects or development projects. These are the kind of things that will come in time, but not just yet.

Practice being a landlord on a smaller project (i.e. a family home or a flat). By doing this, you will be minimising your risk, and it is more likely that you will make less mistakes in the beginning.

Once you are happy with the costs of the refurbishment, be sure to add your contingency onto the works for unknown unknowns. Nobody knows what is going to be unearthed during a refurbishment project, and it is wise to make sure that you have accounted for it in your figures. Once you have this final cost, and the project still stacks up, then it's time to buy the property. We will soon go into more depth about buying the property; however, let's imagine now that the property is yours, and the works can begin.

It is important to keep reins on your budget. Make sure you track everything that you are spending on the project, and keep an eye on the budget plan in order to not overspend and lose money. Once you are into the refurbishment, you will soon realise if your calculations have been correct. It is very easy to spend a little more here and a little more there on items, but they all add up quickly. Be sure to keep a level head, and remember who your target audience is. Do you really need super amazing, crystal door handles, when a basic door handle will suffice? If interior design is not your thing, then be sure to do some research and talk to other investors who may have some knowledge of what is *on trend* and helping to make tenants choose one apartment over another. Magnolia used to be the perfect colour; however, in 2018, a white palette with grey tones is much more desirable. It might be a good idea to drop by at some local new development show homes. They will have chosen top interior designers who are educated and skilled at selling properties; therefore, you can glean their ideas. Also consider looking at topical magazines, Instagram, and Pinterest.

It is important that your refurbishment is done to a good standard so that ongoing maintenance can be minimised, with the least disruption to your tenants. A lot of investors will rip out a kitchen and replace the whole thing. Sometimes the carcasses are good enough, and it is only the doors that need replacing. We suggest using vinyl flooring so that this can easily be replaced if necessary. Floor tiles can be costly upfront and on an ongoing maintenance basis. Tiling the kitchen walls around the work surface areas creates an immediate fresh look to the whole kitchen. It is best to keep the colours simple and neutral. White tiles are inexpensive and can look clean and simple with a different colour border. If a worktop is damaged, it is best to be fully replaced. Any gap or cracks in a worktop are unsightly and unhygienic, and need to be dealt with. By replacing the worktop, the kitchen will look new and fresh for a new tenant.

Check to see what condition the basin and taps are in. They may be just fine, or maybe just a new tap is all that is required. Don't be too quick to chuck everything out. Another area in a single family dwelling that can be easily upgraded is the family bathroom. Sometimes all that is required is a deep clean. The grout can often be discoloured, and mould could have formed, which is unsightly. By replacing grout, or using anti-mould silicone, your bathroom can go from grotty to gorgeous, in a matter of hours. Sometimes the bath is cracked and not functioning properly, and will need to be replaced. Having complete tiled walls does add an additional cost at the beginning of the investment; however, this will reduce overall ongoing maintenance and mould issues. Keep the flooring a simple high quality vinyl that can be replaced as necessary, and make sure that you do not use carpet in the bathroom area. Often, the tenants will use the bathroom as a drying area for their clothes after they have been washed. A good quality extractor fan is a must to avoid condensation problems down the line.

Keep the carpets of a good quality, but do not choose something that is expensive. Keep the colours neutral so that the tenants can add their own splashes of colours with furniture and pictures. It is best practice to put up curtain poles for your tenants. Often, tenants will have their own curtains, and if you don't supply a pole, they will drill all kinds of holes into your new refurbished property, making a pig's ear of it!

By replacing old plug sockets and light switches that are old and tired, it gives the property a clean look overall. Be sure to use a fully qualified electrician for all of your electrical works, and make sure you get electrical and gas certificates. It is simple to replace old lamp shades that are old and ugly. There are some very reasonable priced home depot stores that sell shades for very little money. Sometimes the internal doors have been damaged and will need replacing. Doors, and even seals on broken windows, are fairly low price, and can be easily replaced. We advise that unless you have a real passion for refurbishing properties yourself, and being hands on, that you stick to employing professional trades' people. They will often save you a lot of time in the long run, and the good ones are worth their weight in gold!

We have found that getting referrals from other property investors in the area is the best way to find good tradespeople. Unfortunately, builders often have a bad reputation, maybe it is from media coverage, or maybe the stories are true. We have experienced good and bad trades' people. Remember, your property journey is a marathon, not a sprint. If you have had a bad experience and/or have lost a lot of money with a trades' person, then be sure to draw a line in the sand, move on, and put it down to a great learning opportunity—and be sure to find out where it went wrong, and don't repeat the same mistakes again.

Trust the Figures

"A penny saved is not a penny earned if
at the end of the day you still owe a quarter."
– Mary Landrieu

Let's take a closer look at how to collate and calculate all the figures for your BTL purchase. Once you have done all your research, you are in a position to do a thorough appraisal and calculation of costs for the project. It is here that you will find out the rental yield for your BTL. It is a good idea to use an excel spreadsheet to keep all your calculations together for ease of reference and for adding up. Below are a list of costs that you will need to consider when making a BTL purchase:

Stamp Duty Land Tax – There have been significant changes in the property law in recent years. One of the biggest changes that put a lot of UK investors off, is the changes to how stamp duty land tax charges are structured. Stamp duty is a tax that is paid in the UK, which used to be a flat rate percentage of the price of the property. Since April 2016, if you are buying a second property in addition to your own home, Stamp Duty is required by UK law, at a different higher rate. This is an important factor to consider when calculating the figures in a purchase, as it can have a significant outcome on your profit.

Realistic price that would be accepted for the property – A vendor will usually want to get as much as they can from the sale of their property. To achieve this, normally, they will approach an estate agent to get a market valuation. However, as estate agents are typically commission orientated, they may over-value a property in the hope that it will sell higher than market value, to achieve a higher commission. This can, of course, be counterproductive, as any shrewd purchaser will have done their own due diligence and research to identify as close as possible the real market value. This, in turn, may then cause difficulties in getting a sale, or even getting interested parties through the front door. So, the key here, for any vendor, is to be realistic with your sale price.

Mortgage fees – When you take out a mortgage, you will need to pay a valuation fee and an arrangement fee. There also may be a booking charge and legal expenses. These fees can typically add £2000.00 to your mortgage costs. The *booking fee* can also be known as a reservation fee. This is usually paid upfront when the loan goes through. Just remember that if you don't go through with the mortgage offer presented to you, then you won't get that fee back. The *arrangement fee* is what you pay to set up the mortgage from the lender, and these charges can greatly vary. This can be paid *upfront,* or you can add this cost to your overall mortgage. But remember then, you are paying interest on it over the length of the mortgage product, and this means that this charge will ultimately cost you more. The *valuation fee* is what you pay to the lender for a survey of the property that you are looking to purchase. These costs can vary, depending on what sort of survey you pay for. However, with some mortgages, this fee is incorporated into the mortgage and, therefore, appears to be free.

Legal fees – These are what you pay to a *conveyancing* solicitor for doing their legal paperwork. This includes things like any search fees or stamp duty charges. Usually, they charge a percentage of the mortgage price. There is also a CHAPS fee. This is a cost charged when the lender sends any mortgage funds across to your solicitor.

Finding fee – This is also known as a referral fee. This is simply an amount of money paid to the finder of the transaction. The finder has found the deal, and a commission is paid to bring this deal to the parties involved.

Refurbishment costs – These are the costs or expenses that are associated when you refurbish a BTL. You will need to consult with your tax specialist to identify which expenses are tax deductible.

Deed of guarantee (independent legal advice) – This is a document that is signed in the presence of an independent solicitor not involved in the mortgage offer. The individual(s) are signing to acknowledge that they are legally responsible for any debt that the mortgage may incur. We have had to do this with each loan that we have taken out, even though we purchased each of the properties in our limited company name.

Borrowing costs – Also known as bridging finance, or loan costs, from a family member or friend. This will be a percentage of agreed interest payable either at the end of the loan period or on a monthly basis. Again, this usually is only for a short period while other monies are put into place. If you are unable to repay the bridging loan at the end of the agreed term, you will be hit with high percentage charges.

It is good practice to have a contingency of funds set aside for any unexpected costs. It is easy to skimp on calculations and come up with a ballpark figure, but by doing this, you could easily forget important costs, and under calculate and, therefore, make a loss on the deal. By having these funds available you will safeguard your financial position.

Decisive Due Diligence

"Due diligence is the mother of good luck."
– Benjamin Franklin

Due diligence is not a phrase we were familiar with until we joined our property networking groups. Once we did join, we heard it everywhere, and everyone told us how important it was to do it! We heard it first from Robert Kiyosaki, when we participated in one of his webinars. In fact, until this point in our lives, we had not even attended a webinar. We have now done many since, with different property investing and self development companies.

So what is it exactly? In regards to business and finance, it is a comprehensive and detailed appraisal of a project or deal, BEFORE the deal or project has started. An appraisal is a systematic collation of research and information that is helpful to you, in order to make more informed decisions.

If you have read *Rich Dad Poor Dad,* watched any talks by Robert Kiyosaki, or listened to his podcasts, then you will understand the importance of due diligence and appraisals. Having all the information there is on a deal, helps you to make a better choice of whether to purchase the property or not. The due diligence on buying a property has many different sections to cover. Let's go through each section in a bit more detail:

The local infrastructure now and in the future – These are the basic facilities and systems that are in place that serve an area in a country, city, town, etc. These allow the area to function. We have already mentioned schools, libraries, supermarkets etc. Here are some other facilities to consider. We are talking here about streets, roads, rail, sewer lines, and utility services (i.e. gas, electric, water, telephone, cable, etc.). Some of these are managed by the local authority, and some by private companies. There may be a private or public investment programme coming to your town or city, and there will be published local development plans to reflect these projects. On a downside, it could be that there will be a closure of a facility, and this may actually reduce the prices of properties in that area.

Distances to and from said infrastructure to the investment property – Clearly depending on the location of the property, there will be a reflection on property prices and the amount of interest in a sale. If an area is going to be more popular, then as per the law of supply and demand, there will be more interest, and higher priced properties.

Comparables of similar properties within a ¼ mile, and the last 2 years sold prices – When researching the value of a property, it is useful to draw a ¼ mile radius around the property to see comparables. This will give you an opportunity to look at properties of a similar type, style, layout, and décor, in order to see what price to offer. As a benchmark, it is suggested that you compare sold property prices up to the last 2 years.

The rental prices and demand in the area – Also compare like for like, with rental properties already existing in the area. To get the average rental price in an area, we have researched available rental properties on a search engine. We have added them all together and then divided this number by the number of properties. For example, if you found 20 properties, you add all of their total rental income for a month. Say this is £30,000.00: we would then divide this by the number of properties (20 in this example) to find the average rental income of £1,500.00. You may not intend your property to be average, and you hope that it will be above average; however, by having this figure in mind, it protects you if rentals drop. This will give you a good idea of what to expect.

Profitability – Make sure, after you have done all of your due diligence and appraisals, that you are actually going to be making money. If you calculate it down to the penny, you can work out how long it will take, in months, to get all of your money out of the deal, all things being equal (for example, rents staying the same).

When you buy a property, you need to instruct a surveyor to complete a structural survey in order to ascertain that the property is *sound*, and that there are no structural problems, such as subsidence. The surveyor will also give you a rebuild cost, and this will help you to get a quote for buildings insurance. This will allow you to calculate this cost into your final figures. You must always get a valuation in order to be sure that you are not buying something over the market value. This is even still the case if you are buying a BTL with cash for the total price. It is a document that allows you to go back to the vendor and show them that they are not selling for a fair market value.

Now that you have an overview of where and what to buy, we can delve into the financial aspects and learn how to grow your business.

Chapter 6

Finances

Get Your Finances in Order

"Watch your finances like a hawk."
– H. Jackson Brown, Jr

Are you living paycheck to paycheck? Do you know how healthy your finances are right now? If you are like most people, you *do* live from paycheck to paycheck, relying on the money that you get in from your job, and/or the job of your spouse, to pay for all your expenses and living costs. In this book, we have been showing you that there is another way to live, and to use your assets to give you income instead of working for money. In order to go from where you are today, to having a never ending passive income stream, you will need to be fully aware of your own financial situation. It's vital! It's not the easiest thing to wrap your head around, and numbers and calculations are not everybody's favorite subject. We suggest keeping an asset and liability, incoming and outgoing expense sheet, and to look at your finances at least once a month to know exactly where you stand. We have been doing this for nearly a year now, and we feel a lot more in control of our finances, and can easily see where we are at any given month. Go to our website, www.phillipsrealestate.co.uk/book, to get access to your free bonus assets and liabilities Excel document that will help you track your finances.

On the spreadsheet, you will see a section for all your income streams: work, pension, and passive incomes. Below that is a section to include ALL your outgoing expenses in the month. Consider everything that has gone out of your pocket, including transport, food, housing, clothing, credit or store cards, and socialising. By doing this, you will be able to see how much you spend compared to how much you get in—the idea being to get in a lot more than you spend! Be sure to include your debts, including loans, credit cards, mortgage, etc., and any assets that you own, to see your overall net worth. By doing this each month, you will become more aware of the health of your finances, and be in a better position to make changes if necessary. If you are in debt, then you will need to find ways to increase your income. Look at how you can curb your spending, set up a debt repayment programme, and focus on getting more income—ideally, passive income. You may like the idea of having a holiday, but if it is not going to help you get out of debt, then you will need to hold back until your debts have cleared. If you don't, then you will be making the problem worse, and dragging your debts out for longer. It is about sacrificing a small pleasure today for a better tomorrow. Are there any luxuries that you can cut out? Do you have your nails manicured? Why not cut out this expense and paint your own? Do you spend a lot on going out and socialising? You could consider inviting friends over instead. Have a look through your credit card statement and highlight all these expenses that you could live without. It is a real eye opener to know exactly how much money is going out of your pocket each month, just to *keep up with your lifestyle!* Ideally, you will ultimately want the income from your assets to be paying for all your expenses, and have surplus every month; and this way, you will be financially free.

Once you are in a position where you are making a lot more money than you spend, you can then invest into more assets in order for you to get more passive income. Consider what would happen if, for example, you lost your job due to ill health? We can tell you exactly what would happen, because this is what happened to Jo. We were both working in the Police Service in London, UK, getting a nice healthy wage. We had started a refurbishment on our 4-bedroom house in London, and life was great. We were meeting a rather hefty mortgage liability, spending on 2 cars, food, and other middle class luxuries. Work began to get very stressful for Jo, as she was put into a department of the police that she didn't want to be in... Domestic Violence. With a workload of about 30 cases at any one time, Jo became stressed, and she ended up having a breakdown. This break down triggered something in her body, which then gave her chronic pain and fibromyalgia. On further investigation, she was diagnosed with Ehlers Danlos syndrome. After therapy, Jo tried to return to work but was unable to work part time. Jo was given an ultimatum by the police to either leave and receive a police pension or get sacked due to poor performance. We decided not to fight the decision but to take the ill health pension. This had a cascade of consequences. No longer could we afford the mortgage payments, the holidays, or the luxuries. We had to sell the house and move into a very small two-bedroom house. As you can imagine, this was a very challenging time for us. Take a moment to consider how ill health or redundancy may affect you without having a passive income to support your lifestyle.

The law of attraction dictates that you will not get more money until you learn to handle what you already have. If you can change your mindset from "I can't afford it," to "How can I afford it," it will open up your world to hundreds of possibilities, and help you to be more creative when creating and managing money. Why not give it a go? If you are struggling with money right now, try thinking about all of the different ways that you can get some money to start you off. Be as creative and whacky as you can, as you write down your ideas. One odd or seemingly strange idea could lead to your most brilliant idea to date, so don't hold back. You will be amazed at the different ideas that come up.

Once you have that monthly figure of all your expenses, you now have your figure that you can set as your goal to achieve financial freedom.

This means, once you get passive income of this amount, you never have to work again. Bear in mind that this is your financial freedom goal, not your financial luxury goal, or financial opulence goal. This passive income money would pay for all your bills and outgoing expenses, and would give you the freedom and choice to work IF YOU WANTED TO. You may decide to never work again! You may love your job and don't want to give up work. The important thing here is that you have choice. Now, you will need to work out how many BTL properties you will need in order to get this passive income. Is it 4, 5, or 6, or maybe more in a lower value area of the country?

Borrowing Money the Right Way

"I would borrow money all day long, if the cost of borrowing was less than the expected return."
– Brad Schneider

Money has certainly been a taboo subject in Britain and in many other countries in the world. We hardly get taught about money at school: how to make it, save it, or multiply it. In fact, whilst at the dinner table when she was young, Jo remembers asking her friend's dad how much money he made. Jo was quickly made aware that it was not a subject to discuss at the dinner table!

When you attend property networking events, there is often a section for individuals to stand up and make a pitch. This gives you the chance to speak for about one minute. You can use this time to let attendees there know that you are a property investor, and explain what you do and the opportunities that you can offer. There is strict guidance in relation to receiving funds from sophisticated and high net worth investors, regarding their annual income and their net assets. Please seek financial advice from a professional if you wish to attract these sorts of investors.

The best way that we have found to get started is to approach friends and family for a loan, in which they receive a return on their investment. Remind them of the poor interest that they receive from the banks, and that due to inflation, they may actually be making a loss on their savings. If you can explain to your friends and family about your BTL property deal, then they may be more inclined to lend you the money. Be sure to get a contract drawn up so that your investor is fully at ease, and both parties know where they each clearly stand. This must be done before they transfer any money over to you. In your conversation, ask them what they would like as interest on their money, rather than stating a figure. You may be surprised at how much they are willing to lend, and it will at least give you an anchor point to discuss the matter further. When the loan is due to be repaid, you can invite them to either reinvest the funds, including the interest, give them back the interest only, or give them their money back. To make your investor feel reassured and confident in investing in you, it may be helpful to let them know your track record (if you have one). Be sure to update them with the progress of your projects. It might take a few times in making contact, and explaining to them, so that they fully understand what you are trying to achieve. They may be new to the concept of property investing, and may need to have the options explained to them a number of times so that they feel confident about passing you their money.

Other ways of borrowing money may be by way of a bank overdraft. You will need to discuss this with you bank to fully understand the terms of this facility. Credit cards should be used with caution. They should really only be used for short-term borrowing for buying assets. It is possible to get credit cards that have offers on them that do not charge you any interest in the beginning, and for a set period of time; for example, 0% for 24 months. You really need to have a good strategy to pay these back when the introductory offer comes to an end.

In 2018, personal loans are very reasonable. They can be used to obtain larger amounts of money. Other options include peer-to-peer, crowdfunding, and payday loans. With any of these options, please seek the appropriate financial advice on what is the most suitable for you. We are unable to give any further financial advice, as we are not financially regulated. Debt is not always a bad thing. If it is used correctly, it can be a very powerful tool. It can allow you to improve your quality of life, as it can help you to grow your business. There is good debt and bad debt, and the overriding thing here is to use debt correctly and to know the difference between good and bad debt. Robert Kiyosaki talks a lot about how he loves debt, and we found it initially very hard to understand, as we had grown up to believe that all debt is bad, and that you need to get out of debt to live a happy life. Always have a plan B in regards to borrowing money and being able to pay this loan back. Otherwise, you can find yourself in serious financial difficulty.

The More You Give The More You Get

"The law of prosperity is generosity. If you want more, give more."
– Bob Proctor

So long as you are not in financial debt, it is a good discipline to give money. There may be a charity that you are really passionate about, or maybe someone you know that needs a sponsorship in order to raise money. If you give money in order to receive, then the Universe will not respond. Only once you freely give can you truly, freely receive. It is just the law of nature. Giving and receiving go together, because in order for there to be a receiver, there needs to be a giver, and similarly, in order to give, there must be a receiver.

Another quote that really means a lot to us is from Zig Ziglar: *"You will get all you want in life, if you help enough other people get what they want."* So, if you want more money, give more money; if you want more joy, give more joy; and if you want more peace, give more peace. We recommend that you read the book, *The Secret,* by Ronda Byrne. This has been a very influential book in our journey. The book has sold over 30 million copies worldwide, and has been translated into 50 different languages. It is based on the *law of attraction.* It claims that what you think about, comes about. You thoughts, therefore, can change the world directly, and that if you think about this certain thing, then it will appear in your life. Simply, thoughts create things. Where attention goes, energy flows. Byrne talks about a three-step process of asking, believing, and receiving. The book also talks about how, if you show gratitude and use the power of your mind to visualise things, this will improve your wealth, health, and relationships. If you are not receiving enough love, for example, you need to give more love. This is what is called *the law of reciprocity.* If you give a smile, you will get a smile. If you are lazy, then this law of reciprocity will not reward you.

Bob Proctor, who is presently 84 years of age, is a famous life coach and life mentor, born in Canada, in 1934. He is a motivational and uplifting international speaker, with a vibrant personality. His positive outlook on life is contagious. His agenda has been to help people to aspire to a life of abundance in every way, including having successful relationships, being financially free, and being spiritually aware.

He is the author of over a dozen books, including: *You were born Rich, The Art of Living, Thoughts are Things,* and *It's not about the Money.* He is an inspiration for us, and we love the fact that he reads his own audio books. In his book, *The Seven Power Principles for Success,* you can get the real feel of passion from listening to him speak. He has said the following, in relation to giving: *"This generation we have raised generations of go getters; we've got to raise a generation of go givers."*

Our property partners at Development Discovery support a charity called H Giving. One of the ways that we are able to give back is also to support this charity. Two of our property partners, Pauline Heron and Charles Zhao, are the charity's trustees. This charity aims to effectively and permanently build a sustainable community for orphans in Webuye, Western Kenya. In order to do this for a sustainable future, and for the long term, they need to be firstly set up so that they can be guaranteed to have security, opportunity, and a lifetime of health. It is more than just giving them clothing, sanitation, and food; it is about setting them up for their future. As the saying goes, "Give a man a fish, and you feed him for a day; teach a man to fish, and you feed him for a lifetime." Two of our other partners, Alan Christie and Eduardo Prato, also from Development Discovery, are embarking on a Twin Peak Challenge. This will involve Eduardo running 250km in the Sahara desert, and Alan losing 60kg in weight. We will be sponsoring them per kg/km, and all of the money raised will be going to HGiving.com. This charity relies on donations, and we would encourage you to consider making a donation to this good cause. Please visit www.hgiving.com.

There are so many other great causes; for example, Cancer Research, or NSPCC (The National Society for the Prevention of Cruelty to Children), or the British Red Cross, or the Salvation Army. You may find that you wish to support something that is smaller and closer to your heart, and of course, that is fine as well.

The Transmutation Into Joint Ventures

"Coming together is a beginning; keeping together is progress; working together is success."
– **Edward Everett Hale**

Once you have attended a number of seminars and networking events, you will soon become familiar with the words, *joint venture*. It is essentially when 2 or more people get together on a project, and use each other's skills in order to progress a project and to make money. Imagine for a moment, if you did all your property investing on your own, how long it would take you to buy 1 to 10 investment properties. Consider being able to use someone else's money, while you invest your time and think of the endless possibilities! This is why joint ventures are so popular and worth investigating further.

JVs can be made between two people or two companies. It is generally characterised by the partners sharing ownership, risks, and returns. Companies that have got together, for example, are car manufacturers, Toyota and BMW. They have partnered together to research ultra-lightweight materials, vehicle electrification, and hydrogen fuel cells. NASA and Google developed Google Earth. Sony Ericsson, in both the telecommunication and electronics sector, joined together as well.

Our first hands on experience of a joint venture was with the company, Development Discovery. Development Discovery (DD) is a property development company run by Pauline Heron, Alan Christie, Eduardo Prato, Aidan Heron, and Charles Zhao. Their mission is to educate property developers in order to contribute to providing new homes due to the UK housing shortage. The team have a combined experience of over 100+ years, and they also offer investors a good return on their capital investment. We have embarked on a joint venture with Development Discovery. We enrolled in a 12-month education programme to learn about Houses of Multiple Occupation (HMO). This course was run in and around London, and was comprised of workshops and mastermind days to teach us the fundamentals about HMOs: *legislative requirements, site visits, property analysis and evaluation, identifying suitable properties that have potential, floor plan analysis, meeting expert speakers, commercial to residential conversions and development, pitfalls and problems that can be encountered, and how to complete a project appraisal document.* There was always an opportunity to ask questions, in a safe, relaxed, informal environment.

During the Mastermind days, we gathered together with the other group participants at various hotel conferencing venues. Tea, coffee, and lunch was always supplied. One of the biggest attractions of working with DD, and of their education, was the fact that we would become partners in their company, and we would own 2 HMOs, which we would own with them, 50/50. We were responsible for sourcing the property, and DD was responsible for the finances of the project.

This journey also involved learning how to work with architects, RICS surveyors, and estate agents; obtaining planning permission; meeting with local authority councilors and planning officers; and instructing any other surveys (i.e. noise reports, etc.). It has been a fascinating journey, which we are still on, and we are in the process of buying our first HMO. We are now doing another exciting project with DD, but more of that later, in Chapter 10 of this book.

Joint ventures give you the opportunity to leverage others people's knowledge. It might be that you have the funding but not the knowledge or it might be that you have the knowledge but not the funding. Either way, it is an opportunity to join together in a partnership to help each other. Now that we have retired from the police service, we both have more time, and this is something that we can offer back to our partners. If you are interested in becoming a partner with us and Development Discovery, or if you are looking for a great return on your investment, then please email us at www.phillipsrealestate.co.uk/jointventure

Packaging & Sourcing Deals For Others

"People who wish to go into the future should have two skills to succeed: the ability to deal with people, and the ability to sell."
– Shiv Khera

You might not have a giant pot of capital right now. You might not know the sorts of people that have loads of money—well, not yet anyway! You may be in debt yourself, and feel that there is no way that you could possibly start your own property portfolio. Or you may have one or two properties, and now you have run out of money for your next one. Property sourcing is a fantastic way to gain a lot of insight into good and bad deals, and to get paid for doing your research along the way! *"Why would someone pay me a load of money when they could find deals themselves?"* This was the question that I used to ask. *"Why pay me £3K for just finding you the deal?"* The answer is easy: TIME. It's usually time, although sometimes it is lack of knowledge of an area, or sometimes people are just not good at finding deals, and have no desire to do the research involved in finding a great deal.

A brilliant way to get some capital to start with before you buy your first investment property is to source deals for other people. Once you have attended several networking events, you will have begun to develop relationships with other likeminded investors, and they will always be looking out for great deals. Target those investors you know who have very little time to spare on deal sourcing. Maybe they have a full time job, or kids, or are absorbed in their business. The great thing about deal sourcing is that it is a win-win scenario. They don't have the time, and you don't have the money; therefore, you can help each other to achieve what you both want. You could either just start researching a good location with good yields for property, or you could ask investors their specific criteria. Either way, you can find awesome deals, and people will be more than happy to part with their cash in turn for all the research and information that you have provided.

Consider deal sourcing as an extra income revenue to support your property business. Make sure that the properties that you source are of good quality, great location, near good amenities, and that there is plenty of money to be had in the deal. Try to imagine that it was your own deal, thinking carefully about the tenant profile and what a tenant is looking for out of the property. Consider leafleting in your desired area. When you come to put all your research together, make sure you have all the information that would be required to make a decision on the property. Be sure to have another proposal document that just gives the headlines of the deal to start with. However, on the appraisal, make sure that the document you have is professional, typed up, and includes photos, floorplans, planning, etc., just like your own appraisals. Make sure that when you do the viewing, you take pictures yourself, and don't rely on the photographs that the agent website has. For one thing, they could be out of date, or not capture the true essence of the investment.

Often, agents take photographs in order to enhance the property, and will, therefore, miss the mould on the ceiling in the bathroom, or the repointing that needs to be done on the brick work, or the hole in the roof! Be sure to add all pictures so that the buyer is fully equipped to decide if it is right for them or not. Consider attaching other documents provided by the council about regeneration or plans for the coming years. Be sure to put in a title page and a contents page for ease of reference. You will need to have thoroughly researched the area, and that the information is appropriate to the deal. For example, put information about comparison room rental prices if the property is ideal for renting. Also, put in sold prices of other properties that are within ¼ of a mile of the investment property. It may be useful to put other properties that are for sale in the area, in order to get an idea of what is currently on the market. Bear in mind that those prices are just asking prices, and they do not hold as much value as sold prices, as a vendor can ask whatever price he or she likes for their property! It doesn't mean they are going to sell it for that!

Write down all the important things about the property in an easy to read format. Lists and tables are good for doing checklists. Be sure to note the condition of the property and garden as a whole, and then go into further details about the specifics. It will be useful to the buyer to know how much the refurbishment project will cost. We have only learnt about pricing, and how much things cost, from doing our own projects and from our mentors. At this stage, you may not have done your first project yet; therefore, asking a mentor, or finding builders in the networking groups, is a great way to understand how to price up a refurbishment. Ideally, you can put in all potential costs for the sale and refurbishment so that the buyer can make an informed decision. By doing this a number of times for other people, and getting paid for it, you can soon get a great name for yourself as a quality sourcer, and you will really get to know an area for when you start investing yourself. It will depend on the deal as to what the buyer is prepared to pay you for sourcing a deal. It varies throughout the world and, therefore, advice from a mentor is essential here in order to not undersell your hard work, or to overprice your work and sell nothing. By getting them to sign a nondisclosure agreement (NDA), the buyer that you are speaking to is not at liberty to pass the information onto somebody else. You don't want to have done all that hard work for nothing!

Other Ways to Get Capital

"When you have exhausted all possibilities,
remember this: you haven't."
– Thomas Edison

If you are just starting out, and you don't have a pot of cash to invest just yet, then you will need to be more creative and think of alternative ways to get capital for your first investment property. Here are a few suggestions:

Friends and family – Word will soon get round that you are investing in property. Speak to family and friends to see if they would like to loan you money for your deal or possibly do a joint venture. Ensure that you have a written agreement in place so that there is no ambiguity or confusion about the deal.

Affiliate marketing – This has taken off massively over the past few years and if you have a knack for this kind of thing then it could be quite lucrative indeed. Consider all of the big brands in business that you can sign up to on their affiliate programme. As you market their products and services and when somebody clicks your link and buys, then you make a commission. This could stack up to hundreds, thousands, tens of thousands or much more. If you are interested, then Progressive Property and Wealth Dragons both offer fantastic courses to learn more about affiliate marketing. But remember the key here is to use this money to invest into a property asset in order for you to get a passive income and to build your wealth.

EBay, or car boot sales – Take a look around your house at all of the things that you have bought. Take a moment to consider whether or not you really need them, or whether you would prefer the money to buy assets, now that you have the knowledge and understanding. It may be that you have accumulated a number of mobile phone upgrades over the years. We came across several old phones that we didn't use. They were just sitting there in their original box, collecting dust. It was amazing how much they were actually still worth.

Loft or garage – Maybe you could do with a big clear out. We find this quite a therapeutic way to spring clean. You might think that there is not a lot of money from these small items, but it is amazing how they can all add up. You might have an old record collection stored that you can trade in. There are some specialist shops out there that will buy your whole record collection, as some of your vinyl records may be very collectable and, therefore, worth more than you expected.

Jewellery or watches – Consider old watches or inherited jewellery that you might no longer use or want. It's incredible how much these might be worth. Most high street shopping centres have shops that will buy scrap gold or jewellery.

Stamp collections – Danny used to collect first day cover postage stamps. He subscribed to the British Philatelic Society, which sent out these first day cover stamps every month. What made them of value was the franking on the envelope and stamp, and its mint condition. These were all carefully placed into a presentation binder. Maybe you have collected postage stamps from all over the world. You might have them all quite well organised, with different pages for different countries. This accumulation of numerous stamp books, collected over time, will have developed into a massive stamp collection. Stamps can really be worth a load of money. We'd suggest that you go to a professional valuer who deals with stamps, to get their true value and worth.

Coin and paper money collections – Over the years, Danny was given various commemorative coins as gifts from his grandfather: the Queen Elizabeth coronation coin; Charles and Diana's wedding coin; a set of decimalisation coins, dating back to 1971; and the Queen Elizabeth golden and diamond jubilee commemorative coin. Also, when the Bank of England produced a new pound coin, which replaced the old paper one-pound bank note, this came in a presentation box, which increased the value when Danny sold it. Maybe you have a first edition of an old or new coin, or a mint condition paper money note. These are collectables that have a value, and there will definitely be people out there who will offer you cash in exchange for your collection.

Paintings – Maybe you have redecorated your home, and there is a particular painting, picture, or print that you bought a while ago, which has now ended up in the loft. Wrapped up carefully, hopefully, in bubble wrap or something to have kept it safe, it just didn't fit in with the new decorations. It just might be worth something to someone else. So just leaving it there, again, gathering dust, is not benefitting anyone. Go and have a look now.

Clothes – It's amazing how many old clothes we accumulate, whether it's because of changing fashions or colours and styles, or because you might have gone up a size or down a size. Again, these items are just there; they may be stored in an old box or suitcase, and have been forgotten. Go and get them out and have a look. There are organisations out there that will pay by the weight for clothes, or you can Ebay them if they have a branded label. If you feel charitable, of course, then you could just give them to the local high street charity shop. They are always very appreciative of donations.

Cars – You might have a second or even third car that you don't really use, which is just out there or in the garage. Think of the savings of not having to pay insurance, road tax, MOT (annual vehicle roadworthy inspection after 3 years from new), etc. If the inconvenience is not going to be too impactive on your day-to-day life, then sell it. Could you cope with not having a car at all? If you get enough money together, and buy a property investment asset, consider using the cash flow that is generated to let you lease a new car instead.

If you are brave enough and are feeling generous then consider giving away some of these items as you will be sure to receive back that which you have given and more. It is the law of reciprocity.

So, try to think out of the box, and be creative in other ways of how to make money. In the next chapter, we are going to share some property secrets and fantastic gems of advice that we have learnt along the way. Don't stop reading now, as these will be life changing.

Chapter 7

Tricks and Tips

Join an Association

"I think that we should remember that social change can happen when people join together with some strength."
– Haskell Wexler

We have joined the Residential Landlord Association (RLA) in the UK. Depending on where you are in the world, there will be an association or governing body that you can join, for property investors. The RLA is an organisation especially designed to support landlords. Their website says, *"We provide the expertise, support, and tools you need, so you can do the right thing, by you, your tenants, and the industry as a whole."* They offer training for landlords about finance and tax, renting, regulations, and management, insurance products, etc. We have used the RLA to get a referral to get buildings insurance for our properties. On their website, there are all sorts of documents and guides. As a member, we have access to their telephone hotline. This has been very useful when we became a new landlord, as we were able to call them up and get advice. As a landlord, you can join the RLA accreditation scheme, and they also send out a bi-monthly investor magazine, which is full of great articles and advice about being a landlord. Please go to www.rla.org.uk for further information.

In the UK, the other main organisation that supports landlords is the National Landlords Association (NLA). Their website says, *"Increasing competition, loss of rental income and problem tenants are just some of the issues that you could be facing as a landlord. That is why the NLA offers you access to a range of benefits and services, with comprehensive representation on a wide range of local, national, and international levels."*

The NLA state that they "advise, lobby, and connect." This means that they bring single property landlords together with large portfolio landlords, in order to aspire and drive future development. Some of the benefits of joining the NLA are unlimited access to their expert telephone advice line, discounted rates to some of their courses, and a subscription to their magazine. To get more information about the NLA, go to www.landlords.org.uk.

Both organisations offer very similar services. Their membership prices are also quite similar.

Here is a list of the benefits of becoming a member or a landlord association. So, wherever you are in the world, please consider the following. We would highly encourage you to consider the overwhelming amount of support that you can be given. In any new venture, knowledge is power, and when you are new to being a landlord, like anything new, you don't know what you don't know.

Membership – With your membership, you will have a membership card, and you will have access to use the NLA or RLA logo on your business cards and literature. This can especially be a bonus to tenants. This will give the tenant the reassurance and confidence that you are legitimate and not a rogue landlord.

Tax Investigation Insurance – Understanding also about tax investigation insurance is helpful. Basically, this will offer protection to you as a landlord in case of an HMRC enquiry (Her Majesty's Revenue and Customs is a non-ministerial department of the UK Government, responsible for the collection of taxes). This can save you a lot of money if your accountant needs to represent you or present paperwork on your behalf to HMRC.

Continued Professional Development – It may serve you well as a landlord to consider their accreditation and Continued Professional Development (CPD) courses. There are numerous courses to get up to speed with regulations, laws, and liabilities of a landlord. We would recommend that if you are new to this game that you do your research, and consider attending a course that will allow you to educate yourself in how you can offer quality services to your tenants. The Capital Gains Tax course may give you useful information in understanding the CGT implications for you, and there are other eLearning courses available.

Suppliers & Resources – Both organisations have access to a list of recognised suppliers, and much more. As a landlord, you need to have full access to all information regarding the residential sector, and once you are a member, you can access their range of free or discounted resources.

Tenancy Agreements – Being able to download your own tenancy agreements is a great advantage, as you can be assured that your contract with a tenant is legal and binding, and that it will stand up in court when any disputes arise. This has got to give you peace of mind. There is also an online library for other documentation that you require access to. Once you are a member, tenants may also wish to verify your accreditation. The tenant can also do this by contacting either organisation to feel assured and reassured that you are legitimate.

Tenant Checks – Whenever you get a new tenant, or if it's your first tenant, you will need to do various checks. This will ensure that you are aware of how to correctly obtain either a basic or a fully comprehensive tenant reference check.

Mortgages – You may wish to get advice or a quote on the best buy-to-let mortgage, and both organisations will assist you with access to a broker.

Tenancy Deposit Scheme – You will need to understand what the Deposit Scheme is. Knowing how to fulfill your legal obligations with tenancy deposits is essential to the smooth running of a tenanted property. Remember this is not your money to spend as you wish, there are strict rules and regulations protecting a tenant deposit.

Rent Protection – It can be crippling to a landlord if the tenant does not pay their rent. Clearly, this can be for many reasons, but nevertheless, you may wish to protect your rental income. You will need to know what this insurance will cost, and whether it is worth it for your circumstances.

Inventories – Before a tenant enters your property, it is advisable to have a full property inventory. This will record exactly what the condition is of your property (i.e. the decoration, any marks or damage to the walls, furniture, white goods, etc.). It will also record what else you are leaving inside the property for the use of your tenant.

Property Repossession – There are occasions when you need to retake possession of your property. It is really important at these times that you do this legally; otherwise, you may find that if you unlawfully evict a tenant, that you yourself gets prosecuted. Get advice on how to deal with this properly.

Company or Personal Name

"Decide what you want, decide what you are willing to exchange for it. Establish your priorities and go to work."
– H. L. Hunt

In 2015, it was announced that there would be changes to mortgage interest relief in the UK. At that time, it was unclear how it would affect the landlord. After deducting mortgage interest, you would be taxed 20% as a basic tax payer, and 40% as a higher rate tax payer on any profit. For those with an income of £150,000 or over, the tax rate would increase to 45%. The old rules were that you could deduct your mortgage interest along with any associated fees, and all your other costs, before determining your profit for tax purposes. From April 2017, the change started to take place, and will come into full effect in 2020. The squeeze on profits is another reason why property investors have been in decline and are selling their portfolios, and making other investments elsewhere. This is a fantastic opportunity for the savvy property investor to benefit from. If you start your business using a limited company to purchase your properties, then this piece of legislation does not affect to you. These changes only affect sole traders who buy properties in their own names. It used to be that any interest charged on a mortgage could be deducted and offset against your profit when doing your accounts. This could mount up to quite a lot over a year. After 2020, you will be unable to deduct any mortgage interest from your profits for tax purposes.

There is always plenty of discussion when it comes to owning property in your own personal name, or if it should be owned within a company structure. There are lots of different types of companies that you could consider; for example, a Limited Company, a Limited Liability Partnership (LLP), Public Limited Company (PLC), and others. You will need to take the time to fully understand the consequences of each of your options. There is not a right or wrong answer, as some may have you believe; rather, it is what is right for you, your family, and your own personal circumstances. The UK government is looking to professionalise the industry and crack down on rogue landlords. On the 6th April 2018, a live UK National database of landlord offenders was published. These landlords will have been convicted of a range of housing, immigration, and other offences; for example, unlawful eviction, fire and gas safety offences, and the leasing of overcrowded properties.

Heather Wheeler, Minister for Housing and Homeless, said, *"I am committed to making sure people who are renting are living in safe and good quality properties. That's why we're cracking down on the small minority of landlords that are renting out unsafe and substandard accommodation.....landlords should be in no doubt that they must provide decent homes or face the consequences."*

Some landlords will face a banning order, ranging from 12 months to life, preventing them from renting property. We decided early on that we wanted to purchase properties under a *limited company* name, and Phillips Real Estate Ltd. was born, in 2017. We had previously owned another business, and were familiar with the limited company structure and responsibilities. It is really only once you have committed to a path that you see how the business runs. For us, we are able to keep the business separate from our personal finances; for example, having a bank account for personal, and a bank account for business. If we needed to buy something for our properties, we would use our business credit card. Our personal transactions would be purchased on our personal credit cards. We now know the rules and regulations to follow, but it was initially a steep learning curve to get it right. We were advised that a limited company is the best structure and most efficient for taxes, in our situation.

Let's have a look at the actual costs of the transaction of buying in your own name, vs buying in a company name. We have just obtained a mortgage with Aldermore Bank. We have refurbished it to a reasonably high specification, and now the property is tenanted. We wanted to see how much seed capital we could actually get out of the property. The property was bought in a limited company name, and the mortgage, therefore, was for a limited company. Here are the items to consider that you will have to pay for: property valuation (required either way), mortgage arrangement fee, legal fees from Aldermore Bank, solicitor fees plus disbursements, independent legal advice, personal guarantee, and stamp duty. The interest rates for a limited company mortgage are always higher. In both cases of either purchasing as an individual or as a limited company, there is still the cost of stamp duty to be paid. Also, when you come to the end of your mortgage product term, you will incur these costs again if you go to another bank or mortgage company. Bear in mind that if you choose to buy properties in your own name, and then later on decide to change to a limited company, there will be additional taxes to pay for doing so; for example, capital gains tax and stamp duty.

Professionalise Yourself

"To me, business isn't about wearing suits or pleasing stockholders. It's about being true to yourself, your ideas and focusing on the essentials"
– Richard Branson

Consider what it means to you to be a professional. Does it mean that you need to do a good job, or be smartly dressed at work? Does it mean having your educational degrees displayed on the wall in your office for clients to see? Maybe it includes all of these. We think that there is much more to being a professional than just these. In any type of business, there are certain characteristics that you would need to make you truly professional.

Competency – You will need to educate yourself and achieve industry professional qualifications. A talent you can strive to achieve is to be resourceful and skillful, and show understanding.

Reliability – Always be on time for meetings. Deal with issues promptly, and always get the job done as promised. Be honest and upfront if you are unable to keep to your commitment. This will show your trustworthiness.

Appearance – Always consider being appropriately attired to meetings. Make sure that you always look clean, neat, smart, and fresh.

Demeanor – How you conduct yourself will give a lasting impression to your peers and clients. Be mindful of your mannerisms, tone of voice, and how your mood comes across. Being polite and speaking with clarity is essential.

Organisational Skills – Always be able to find, easily and quickly, whatever is needed, and have a well organised work environment and appropriate systems in place so that, at any appointments, you have everything at hand.

Poise – Remain calm in all situations, even when the going gets tough. Resorting to the same sort of argumentative behaviour as a client or customer is going to be unhelpful. So keep your cool, and try and be balanced and tactful.

Attitude – Some professionals (e.g., doctors, solicitors, lawyers, therapists) are bound by their code ethics. Even if you don't have such a code, be sure to show ethical behaviour at all times. Having these morals will portray a good attitude and give your reputation credibility.

Phone manner – Always be polite and friendly, and be sure to truly listen to the other person. Be attentive and courteous, and ensure that you have clarity. Summarising the conversation can help to let the other person know that you understand what has been said.

Correspondence – When you are writing an email or letter, it is best practice to be succinct and to keep to the point. Be sure to let the other person know what you want and what you are trying to achieve. Be friendly but not too informal with your tone.

Accountable – You need to be able to prove to someone else that the task at hand has been completed as promised. If you make a mistake, own up to it immediately, and take responsibility to resolve the issue at hand. Even if someone else has messed up, don't blame others, but take on the responsibility to resolve the problem.

With all of the above in mind, you also need to be branded. We would suggest that you have a corporate identity. To achieve this, you will need a company logo. We used www.logoshines.co.uk. You can then use this logo for business cards, a company letterhead, and email footer. Having a professionally designed website with photographs and great content will help you to stand out from the crowd. Have a biography section, and feature any qualifications, experience, and projects that you have completed or are working on. You can also put links to your joint venture partner's websites. We used Sally Munden, at www.banburywebdesign.com. Sally is fantastically creative, coming up with interesting and innovative designs, and she can adapt your website to suit your needs. We highly recommend her. We had our headshots done by www.davidjohnheadshots.com. We would really recommend David, a true professional who will make you feel at ease—and you will get some natural, great shots.

Reshaping Your Organisation

"The best preparation for tomorrow is doing your best today."
– H. Jackson Brown, Jr.

Very early on, we found ourselves becoming overwhelmed with everything we needed to do to start our property journey. We were overwhelmed by the knowledge, emails, meetings, and to-do tasks. It was only some way into our property journey that our mentor advised us to use *Asana*. This is a free business management application, available on IOS and Android. We were advised to consider using this app for scheduling everything to do with property, and especially our to-do list. At that time, we had already signed up to another mentorship programme, in which they began using *Basecamp,* which has a similar function. Suddenly, we had 2 very good systems to choose from. We settled with Basecamp in the end because it was easy for us to communicate with our joint venture partners, who were already using this product.

"Basecamp, formerly named 37signals, is a privately held American web application company based in Chicago, Illinois. The firm was co-founded in 1999, by Jason Fried, Carlos Segura, and Ernest Kim, as a web design company." – Wikipedia

As mentioned previously, Basecamp allows you to systemise teams and projects, and to invite other users to share, contribute, and participate in a project. Access all of your documents all in one place. There is no need to use multiple systems or ways of working, like keeping ideas and to-do lists in note books or on stickies, or getting emails lost in the system. Everyone who has been invited to the project will see what exactly everyone else sees. This way is clear and transparent, time saving, and efficient. If there is a lead on a project, they can assign tasks to individuals or groups, and so involving the right people as required. We have found Basecamp to be very helpful, and each project is a rental property. This gives us the flexibility to keep all records to do with a property in one easy accessible place. All the refurbishment details can go into one folder. Property Management can all go into another folder. During our refurbishments, we have logged all our email conversations, which can be imported into a specific project. We used the to-do list during the acquisition process, and could prioritise and tick off tasks once that particular stage had been completed. There are other functions, which we are yet to explore. By putting all our work for our property investments under one cloud based digital system, it frees our mind and gives us reassurance, as we are in control. We can access the system on any PC, Mac, IPad, laptop, and even on our phones.

Another fantastic system we use is Xero. *"Xero is a New Zealand-based software company that develops cloud-based accounting software for small and medium-sized businesses."* – Wikipedia

Don't make the mistake of thinking that this looks easy, and then try and use it yourself. If you are serious about property investing and taking your life to the next level, then employ a bookkeeper who is knowledgeable in this accounting software. Xero is a simple and effective tool in your toolkit, and beats an excel spreadsheet by a million percent, even if you are just starting out. Xero tracks daily expenditure within the company, with a facility to include copies of receipts so that everything is digitally recorded and up to date. This also avoids the requirement or need to store these receipts. However, please consult your accountant for best practice.

Gone are the days where you are dreading the end of year's tax accounts, where you are scrambling around trying to remember what payments were for what. Xero gives you the freedom to see at a glance the financial health of your company. You can assign purchases to projects, and rental incomes to specific properties, in order to see how well, overall, they are cash flowing. There is a monthly subscription cost after a 30- day free trial, and this is worth every penny. If you do have other businesses, you are able to (with one login in) toggle between them, and restrict access to individuals whom you don't wish to have access. When you are out at a business meeting, and incur costs at a restaurant or coffee shop, for example, it is easy to just get out your phone and use the Xero app. You can *zapp* the receipt, which stores it, ready for your bookkeeper to make the appropriate expenses entry. Mileage, or train or rail travel expenses, can also be recorded, and there is a copy function for repeated journeys, rather than having to rewrite from fresh each time.

Property Acronyms Explained

"Overcome your barriers, intend the best, and be patient. You will enjoy more balance, more growth, more income, and more fun."
– Jack Canfield

Wow, what a minefield. When we started learning about investing property, there was so much jargon. We couldn't understand a lot of what people were saying. It was like we were learning a foreign language. We thought it would be useful to add a section in this book about the different language that we've learnt during our journey. Here are some of the acronyms that we have come across:

AST – Assured Shorthold Tenancy – This is an agreement between you, the landlord, and the tenant.

ARLA – Association of Residential Letting Agents – When we were completing our HMO proposal document, we needed to establish if the agent was a member of ARLA.

B2L/BTL – Buy to let – This is normally a residential property for which you take a buy to let mortgage out on. This mortgage can be sourced from a mortgage broker. This type of property is a safe way of making an investment, as it will give you cash flow on a monthly basis, after the mortgage and other expenses have been paid.

BTR – Build to Rent – These are properties built specifically for the rental market.

BMV/BFM – Below Market Value or Below Fair Value – This is the price of a property that is believed to be below current prices in that area.

DIP – Decision in principle – When you request a mortgage, the broker will let you have a loan in principle, where they will lend you a certain amount based on some basic information.

EPC – Energy Performance Certificate – This is needed for properties when let, sold, or constructed. It provides details of energy performance at the property, and what you can do to improve it.

ERC – Early Repayment Charges – This is the amount of money that you need to pay to the lender if you wish to sell the property before the end of the term.

GCH – Gas Central Heating – A gas fired water system that is used to centrally heat the property radiators and give hot water to your taps.

GDV – Gross Development Value – The amount of money that the whole development costs.

HMO – House in Multiple Occupation – This is a property rented to at least 3 people who don't know each other. Kitchens and bathrooms may be shared. Licensing may be required now.

IFA – Independent Financial Advisor – This independent advisor can give independent advice and can sell financial products from across the market.

JV/JVP – Joint Venture/Joint Venture Partner – an arrangement between 2 parties or more to pool their resources to achieve a specific goal.

LHA – Local Housing Authority – A local government department responsible for the costs of facilities and public services.

LTV – Loan to Value – A financial term that lenders express to the ratio of the loan to the price of the property.

MCOL – Money Claim Online – An HM Courts & Tribunals internet based service for claiming money against defendants.

NLA – National Landlord Association – UK landlord association that gives advice, training, and support to landlords.

OIEO – Offers in Excess of – It is expected that you will offer above that price indicated on the property sales documentation.

OPM – Other People's Money – To use money from other people to fund your deals.

PCM – Per Calendar Month – Is written after the rental figure, in order to let your tenants know that you want to be paid on a monthly basis.

POA – Price on Application – Often seen on price lists or advertisements. You will need to contact the agent to get the price.

RICS – Royal Institute of Chartered Surveyors – a worldwide, professional body dealing with construction, infrastructure, property, and land.

RLA – Residential Landlord Association – UK landlord association giving advice, training, and support to landlords.

ROI – Return on Investment – The ratio between the net profit and cost of investment.

RTR – Rent to Rent – You rent someone else's property with a view to make an improvement, and then rent it out for more than you are being charged. This works well with SA (see below).

SA – Serviced Accommodation – A fully furnished property available for short or long term rental. Offering similar hotel services, such as housekeeping, laundry service, etc.

SDLT – Stamp Duty Land Tax – A government tax when you buy property or land over a certain price.

SSTC – Sold Subject to Contract – A term used when a price has been agreed, subject to a contract being completed.

SVR – Standard Variable Rate – This is the amount of interest that your mortgage rate will return to once the term of your mortgage product has ended.

We hope that this has assisted you in understanding some of the meanings of these acronyms. Now you are better equipped and able to talk to other property investors without feeling intimidated.

Jargon and Buzz Words

"An investment in knowledge pays the best interest."
– Benjamin Franklyn

Here are some phrases we have also come across:

Portfolio Landlord – A landlord or investor who owns 4 or more mortgaged BTL properties. When you come to buy another property with a mortgage, as a portfolio landlord, you will have the entire portfolio assessed by any prospective lender, prior to the provision of the mortgage. Lenders will look at the following:

• business plan
• current cash flow forecasts
• tax liabilities from your rentals
• your experience in property
• your borrowings across the mortgaged properties, and your total income

When applying for a mortgage as a portfolio landlord, you will need to prove additional evidence to support any future debt required. These changes are relatively new, so it is best to speak to a qualified mortgage broker to get the up to date requirements.

Equity Loans – This type of loan is often overlooked but can be a fantastic source of capital to get you started in buying your first investment property. A home equity loan is very similar to your mortgage for buying your own home. If you have enough equity built up, then you may be entitled to this type of loan. But beware the mortgage company will use your home as collateral if you fail to keep up your repayments. You will need to be sure that you can afford the monthly repayments. The rates on this type of loan are generally quite reasonable, especially compared to something like a credit card. They work in the same way as a traditional mortgage, and you will need to get a valuation. Be sure to calculate all the hidden costs, and consider these elements when buying your investment property.

Bridging Finance – Bridging finance is a loan, and should be only used or considered as a short-term finance solution. It is often used as a stop gap whilst you obtain other finance. For this reason, the interest rates can be extremely high, but it's not just the interest that you need to calculate when considering this type of finance. You also need to consider the following charges:

- Valuation fee
- Original loan
- Exit fee
- Facility fee
- Legal fee
- Solicitor arrangement fee
- Deed of personal guarantee fee

Do not be under an illusion that this is a cheap option, even if it is for a few months. The bridging company will also have a *charge* on your property. This means that if you default in your monthly repayments, then they can force the sale of the property in order to get their money back. This loan is typically used for periods of up to 6 months but can be extended to 12 months. If you do not repay at the end of the loan term, you will be faced with even higher rates of interest. Typically, it is possible to obtain a bridging loan over a matter of days, depending on the lender that you use. However, the process can take weeks to complete.

Angel Finance – An *angel* is an investor who is a high net worth individual. They have access to personal disposable finance, and they will make decisions on how they wish to invest their capital. This investor will not be just bringing money to the table; they will also be bringing their experience, contacts, and knowledge. They will want, in exchange, an equity stake in your project. You will need to specify, in any legal contract with your angel, the exact period of time for which they are happy to loan you this money. Or it may be that they are willing to remain in the deal until the end of the specific project. There are financial regulations that you need to adhere to in order to take up angel finance. This protects both the angel and the entrepreneur when investing in a project. An angel investor will need to have self-certified themselves as a *High Net Worth* or *Sophisticated* investor, as defined by the Financial Conduct Authority (FCA). This is advanced stuff, and you will need to know a lot more about this subject if this is something that you are interested in. We came across this phrase early on in our journey, when we attended property network events.

Flip – This is an American term for buying a house, refurbishing it, and then selling it on for a profit. The only problem with this is that it does not become an asset, and you are continually working to get your next capital lump sum. Although this is a great way to get a chunk of capital, and it is something we would like to do in the future, for now, we are going to stick to buying assets that give us cash flow.

Passive Income – This is the sweet spot. This is money that you don't have to work for on a continual basis. You work once, and you get paid forever. A fantastic thing about property is that it allows you to have a passive income, and it will increase over time as rents go up and property prices increase. It is a win-win. It might not seem much at first, but once you have bought a few properties, you will soon see the compounding effect.

Warren Buffett said, *"If you don't find a way to make **money** while you **sleep**, you will work until you die."*

Have a think about all of the different ways that you can create passive income. Here are some ideas to get you started:

- Write a book
- Create an online course
- Rent out a room in your house, or rent out your garage or driveway
- Affiliate marketing

We have given you some fantastic tips and tricks here in this chapter. But stay tuned, because this next chapter is even better, where we talk about some amazing, powerful rules that will put you ahead of the game.

Chapter 8

6 Rules to Live By

Shiny Penny Syndrome

"Successful people maintain a positive focus in life, no matter what is going on around them. They stay focused on their past successes rather than their past failures, and on the next action step they need to take to get them closer to the fulfilment of their goals rather than all the other distractions that life presents to them."
— **Jack Canfield**

Have you heard of *the shiny penny syndrome*? We had no idea what this meant. In fact, when someone first told us, we pictured lots of pennies, all in the room, shining at us, and us not knowing which one to pick. This is kind of what it's like. You get presented with all of these different property deals, and all the different ways you can make money, and you get so excited looking at all of these differences that you don't even know what to focus on. It's almost like being a child in a sweet shop. We would go along to a meeting, and the speaker would talk about how exciting his particular property deal was, and we figured we could do the same. Then we would attend a different seminar where they were talking about a different strategy, and we would get excited about that too. Then we would attend a webinar, and we would see someone making loads of money from another strategy. We thought this would be the best thing for us to do too. It was only when our mentor said to us that we have *shiny penny syndrome*, and that we needed to focus, that we realised what was happening to us.

Don't get me wrong; we think education is key. But there's a lot of content out there. There's a lot of people telling you about how to make money by doing certain things, and it isn't always in your best interest. There are a lot of *get rich quick* schemes too, but property investing isn't one of them; however, if you are persistent, then it is a *get rich* for sure. We found that by reading a certain book, it would recommend another book within the book (much like we have done), and before long, you can find your reading list quite extensive. The same happens if you begin to follow certain people on social media— for example, Bob Proctor, Robert Kiyosaki, Tony Robbins, and Rob Moore—and all of a sudden, you have got hundreds of podcasts, and hundreds of YouTube videos that you want to watch. At one stage, we were receiving so many emails each day from the various people and courses we had signed up to, that it became overwhelming, and we had to cut back and unsubscribe to a lot of them. We did have a folder of emails that we would read later but just never got round to it. We suggest that you stick to a handful of people to learn from, who are reputable and that align with your philosophy in life.

You may well find, as we did, that you get information overload, and often, this information was conflicting. Some people like to use debt to finance their property deals, and tend to use interest-only mortgages; and other people prefer to pay the debt down and use a repayment option. The choice is yours, but we prefer the idea of using debt, much like the Rich Dad philosophy. We all know someone who jumps from project to project, in the hope that the next thing will be the *next best thing,* and make them lots of money. In the property investing world, we have found that there are lots of opportunities to invest your money in different property strategies. We have also discovered that other various courses are offered with promises of great return on investment, especially when you attend free seminars. It is all too easy to fall into the trap of throwing your money into these courses, and spreading the net wide. All of these courses are *shiny* and attractive in the moment, but as hard as it may be, we suggest to stick with your buy-to-let strategy for the first year, to get a solid foundation of passive income before investing in other things. Focus is key. Once you have mastered your buy to let strategy, it will give you the confidence and capital to invest in some of these other strategies.

There are a lot of free seminars that provide excellent education, but be aware that there is no such thing as a free lunch, and that it is a marketing strategy for the companies that offer their courses. These seminars are extremely vibrant and encouraging, and give you a feeling of optimism. You will find great contacts with likeminded people, who will often have done some of the courses that are often being offered by very high profile and wealthy property investors, and these people are very competent public speakers. They can *rev up* an audience, offer incentives, and offer discounts that are only available on the day. Be mindful that a lot of these opportunities are available, certainly later on in the year. There are courses on property investing, purchasing an HMO, mastering money, Amazon affiliate, property development, how to write your own book (we took this one up), stock market mastery, investment in gold and silver, serviced accommodation, rent to rent, public speaking, trading in precious stones, buying repossessed properties, online branding, how to create other passive income, etc. These are all fantastic opportunities, and you will need to select when the best time is for you. We have spoken to some people who have done so many courses that they now have no money left to invest.

You never stop learning; there is always another course to go to. We recently signed up for a webinar on deal sourcing. This free webinar led to a half-day seminar, and this led to a 3-day course. We are not saying that this is necessarily a bad thing, but be aware that the course provider will be looking to sell you the next steps, and you will not always get all of the information you need on the first course.

Feel the Fear and Do It Anyway

"Start by doing what's necessary; then do what's possible; and suddenly you are doing the impossible."
– Francis of Assisi

It is not fear that you have to get rid of. It is not a matter of saying over and over in your mind that it's only fear, and that you should get over it. Rather, it is to face that fear head on, and realise that you have the ability to act in spite of fear—that is the remarkable thing. Seeing, smelling, and feeling the fear in a given situation IS frightening. By acting quickly and taking *the time* out of the fear, and just getting on with it, you can bypass most of the negative thoughts that might automatically pop into your head. It's all too easy to feel frightened about being a landlord, dealing with tenants, handling money and legal documents, making sure that you have all the necessary paperwork signed, etc. If you think about it too long, it can make you freeze or walk away from your dreams. In order to stop the fearful thoughts creeping in, you have to just get on with it. Don't think too much about it—just embrace it. Taking that first step is the beginning of your future.

You may feel more relieved to know that it is not just you that is in fear. This fear that is causing you stress and distress, is something quite natural and very common. If, for example, you have an important meeting or an interview to go to, how do you conquer your fear so that you get there on time, present yourself appropriately, and leave the right impression that is required?

This is all done with preparation. *"Fail to prepare; prepare to fail."*

- Plan your route/journey.
- Choose the appropriate attire.
- Ensure that you are educated and forewarned about the content of the meeting.

- Get there in plenty of time.
- Plan some questions that you are going to ask.

These simple steps show that you can do it and that you can succeed. There have been lots of people in this same position. They have been successful, and you can be too. Repetition is also a great way of dealing with your fear. If there is something that particularly freaks you out—maybe it's travelling on the bus or train to get to appointments—then maybe, if you do not have an alternative mode of travel, easing yourself into these frightening environments when it's quieter might work for you. Not many people go on these transport systems really early. Try it out, and gently make your start time later and later, until you become more accustomed to the journey and your fears. Having some sort of distraction is great. Lots of people use headphones and listen to music or podcasts, etc. Whenever we travel on the train or bus, we leverage our time by listening to audiobooks, and so use the time to educate myself. Playing the book at x1.5 speed or x 2 speed will get you through the book more quickly, and will save you even more time.

We had a very important property planning, pre-application meeting with our planning officer and our architect. It was our first time ever going to such a meeting in our property journey. Before the meeting, we met with the architect, discussed what we were going to say, prepared some points, printed off the professional architect drawings and specifications, dressed up smartly, and got to the meeting reception nice and early. Our fear was that the property we wanted to receive planning permission for was on the ground floor and was commercial. We wanted to convert it to residential. If this could not be achieved, then the whole project would not be viable and would fall apart. The planning officer maybe saw that we were nervous, and immediately allayed our fears that there would not be a problem with making this change of ground floor use at the property. In fact, the issue that he was more concerned with was the fact that the building was adjacent to a restaurant, and that there may be noise to residents from the external restaurant flue. We had not even considered this issue. This actually meant that we would just need to rejig the plans and put any residential areas to the other side of the building. This particular HMO project needed the support of local councillors and local residents. We were advised to engage with the councillors and to meet with them to explain our project. Fear started to set in. The first thing we did was to take action, and then we devised a strategy.

- Research who the ward councillors are.
- Phone the councillors and plan a face-to-face meeting.
- Present our project.

We identified who the local councillors were, and established that one of them had been a mayor of the town, and that he had also sat on the local council building planning committee. Contact was made via phone, and we coordinated a meeting for a few weeks ahead. We then put together prospective plans and architect drawings into a presentation document folder. On the day, we presented our proposals with a laptop and projector, in a PowerPoint presentation, with pictures of the building, current plans of layout, and our proposed drawings. A copy of all of the notes for the presentation was also given to the councillors. We were both really nervous, but we took the bull by the horns, took a deep breath, and went for it. The meeting went really well and had a very positive outcome. The main reassurance was that we wanted to transform a local, iconic, unoccupied building into a home for a number of people. We showed clearly that we did not want to make any structural changes to the exterior of the building, and that the proposed interior build changes and occupants would bring back some life to the old, disused building. We were delighted, and so were the councillors.

Nelson Mandela said, *"I learned that courage was not the absence of fear, but the triumph over it. The brave man is not he who does not feel afraid, but he who conquers that fear."*

Cause and Effect

"According to the Law of Cause and Effect, every effect must have a cause. In other words, everything that happens has a catalyst; everything that came into being has something that caused it. Things don't just happen by themselves."
– Ray Comfort

During our educational journey, we have met Raymond Aaron. Raymond is a Canadian with over 40 years' experience as a motivational speaker, coach, and mentor. His ambition is to teach individuals how to completely change their lives for the better. His strategy is to assist people to *tap into their own potential*. He has written a number of books, and he is a *New York Times* top 10 bestselling author. His titles include *Chicken Soup for the Parent's Soul, Double Your Income Doing What You Love, and Branding Small Business for Dummies*. Also, he is an avid adventurer who has completed the Polar Race. This is a 350-mile foot race to the magnetic North Pole. Raymond has inspired us to dream bigger and to think outside of the box. The way that he did this was to make us more aware of how the physical and spiritual worlds are made up. The physical world is made up of *matter, energy, time,* and *space*. None of these feature in the spiritual world.

We came to understand that everything around you—your home, your car, your clothes, people, belongings, etc.—all came about in your physical world because you conceived them in your mind in your spiritual world. So, what struck us here was that everything that you think about in your spiritual mind, you can actually bring into your physical world. This mindset supports the teachings of the book, *The Secret,* which we mentioned earlier. *The Secret* talks about the law of attraction, and having a positive mindset. On our transformational retreat in Costa Rica, Raymond taught us about *cause and effect*. His perspective was that in life you should be *at cause*. People in the world who live their lives *at cause* are the most successful and rich people.

Do you want to be in the top 3% of people in the world that are *at cause*? Or do you want to remain in the bottom 97% of people in the world? Then you need to take control of your life, and to choose your end result. You need to live from a position of personal power and authority. When *at cause*, you make things happen in your life by accepting personal responsibility for all of your outcomes. You must have the mindset and belief of *"I can do it."* Therefore, you are responsible for what happens in your life, and that you will learn from your mistakes.

Being *at effect* is having the mindset of *"I can't do it."* This means that things will happen to you, or that you are being a victim of circumstance. You are the kind of person who does not take personal responsibility, and will blame other people for all of the things that happen to you. When you live *at effect*, you generally live life feeling fearful, and believe that you do not have control or power over what happens to you. Being *at effect* is living life as a victim, and this will further attract negativity in your life. This can have a compounding effect on everything that happens to you if you don't take responsibility. If you blame the traffic for being the reason for delaying you at an appointment, or if you blame the train delay for you not getting to work on time, these are all examples of not taking responsibility, and of living life as *a victim*; and, therefore, not being *at cause*. If you turn this round the other way, and take personal responsibility for being late—for example, if you had got up earlier or had taken a different route, you would not have been involved in the traffic jam; or if you had taken a different train, then you would have arrived on time—then this is all about being *at cause*. You choose which mindset you prefer.

Raymond introduced us to *postulates*. He told us that if you want something, then you need to postulate it. Essentially, this similarly is about having the positive mindset that if you think something, then it will appear in your life. As there is no *time* in the spiritual world, there is no way of knowing when this postulate will materialise in the physical world, and it might not materialise exactly how you expect it. Raymond invited us to write down 3 postulates that would materialise in our world. The exercise was that he wanted to demonstrate how— if these *simple* things could come true—we could trust that *bigger* things would also come true. Raymond went on to explain that it's not the size of the postulate; it's how much you believe. At the time, we were at a remotely located hotel, where there were no shops or houses or other people, other than the residents at the hotel nearby. Jo wrote down that she wanted the following:

- To have some chocolate
- To be given a book about beliefs
- To see a cat

Within 2 hours, all 3 postulates came true, without any persuasion.

On another occasion, back at home now, Danny decided to postulate that he wanted to receive £60,000.00, to be given to us to fund a property project. Within a week, one of our property friends offered us that exact amount of money to finance the project. We were ecstatic! Now, when we want something to come into our lives, we postulate. Why don't you try it? You have to really believe that it will come to you, and you have to trust this.

We have to say that we were skeptical of this at first, and we were trying to find holes in the theory; however, the more we looked into it—the more we let go and just tried it—the better we felt. It was the incredible empowerment that we felt that made us sit up and take notice. If we had caused "X" in our lives, then how could we change our lives so that "X" does not occur again. It makes sense that if we want something to change in our lives, then we need to take responsibility before moving on to the next step.

Live In The Now

"No matter how hard the past, you can always begin again."
– **Buddha**

Have you ever tried meditation or mindfulness? Maybe you meditate already, and dedicate yourself to being *in the moment* at all times. For some of us, it is a journey of trial and error, and for most people, it is nonexistent!

We had obviously seen and heard about meditation through the years, but we had never really understood the power that comes from it. In fact, we put it in the same category as those weird shops with incense, healing gemstones, and tarot card readings, so never really looked much further.

When we first met, we soon realised that we were two very different types of people. Danny likes to just get on with things, and is an action taker. Jo, on the other hand, likes to plan everything and to systematically check things off in order of priority. Danny is very good at living in the here and now. Jo, on the other hand, is a *holistic* thinker, and can flit from past to future and back, in moments, looking at the bigger picture. Both have their place, and it is clear that we work well and complement each other's strengths. But neither of us practiced mindfulness or meditation.

It was not until her early 30s that Jo came to learn and practice mindfulness. Jo was getting some therapy at the time, as she was going through some stress at work and in her personal life. Whilst within a group therapy, Jo remembers that she was asked to sit still with her eyes closed, and to just *be*, and to witness all her thoughts. Well, she could hardly bear the silence, opening one eye, looking around to see if others were doing this *mindfulness* stuff. Then, within a couple of minutes, Jo could not bear her overwhelming thoughts, and bolted for the door! It was really too hard for her to sit and observe her thoughts. Up until that point, Jo thought that she was her thoughts, and if she thought something bad, then she was bad. Jo didn't understand that a thought was just a thought! It was a massive revelation to Jo as her therapist began to explain to her what mindfulness is. Having been brought up to believe that even if you thought about stealing something, it held as much weight as the *sin* of stealing itself, there was no distinction. As you can see, there was a lot of therapy to be done!

The practice of mindfulness is incredibly important, along with grounding, and we encourage you to try it if you haven't already. Simply sit down and *be*. Shut your eyes and try to list all the different things that you can hear. You will soon be aware of all the different sounds that are happening *now*. Be aware of your thoughts, and try to detach from them; for example, *I wonder what I can cook for supper tonight*. Observe the thought, let it come, and then let it go. Do not engage with it by thinking further... spaghetti Bolognese or chili. It often helps to imagine your thoughts sitting on a cloud, and then watching the cloud float by. Have a go now. Put the book down. Other examples are of putting the thought on a train, but this never worked, as Jo was always too interested in the visual aspects of the train, and got distracted. Find what works for you, and that will only be through trial and error. As the weeks went on, Jo was able to extend the length of time that she was able to be in the moment and to be mindful. This technique works especially well if you are overwhelmed or anxious. It might seem counter-productive to stop what you are doing and to do nothing, but it will help to give you calmness and clarity of thought, at a time that you need it the most.

"What we are today comes from our thoughts of yesterday, and our present thoughts build our lives of tomorrow: our life is the creation of our mind." – Buddha

We have recently embarked on a 21-day mindfulness meditation programme, through Deepak Chopra and Oprah Winfrey. Each morning, before we even had breakfast, we would listen to the session of the day, and let our minds relax and focus on a mantra that Deepak would suggest. We found these sessions deeply relaxing; they gave us a feeling of calm and set us up for the day. There are numerous similar types of meditation techniques. Do your own research and find one that suits you.

"There are no extra pieces in the universe. Everyone is here because he or she has a place to fill, and every piece must fit itself into the big jigsaw puzzle." – Deepak Chopra

Have you ever been around those types of people who are constantly living in the past, replaying tales from old, and who are never actually living but just going on about what they did!? Or maybe you know a *dreamer,* who for years has been talking about the future, and his wonderful plans and ideas, but never seems to get there. Remember, tomorrow never comes… because once the day starts, there is a new tomorrow. The only place to live your live is *today*—the only time to live your life is *now*!

Just living for the now, you become completely centred on where you are at. Live where your life is, and not where it has been, or where your life's journey has taken you. Don't be worried or fixated on where your life may take you in the future. It will not help to worry about the future. If you concentrate your thoughts on *now*, you will be able to deal with what life presents to you.

Developing Your Self-Confidence

"Belief in oneself is incredibly infectious. It generates momentum, the collective force of which far outweighs any kernel of self-doubt that may creep in."
– Amiee Mullins

Have you ever noticed when you surround yourself with positive, likeminded people, you feel somehow empowered? Have you ever had a training day at work where you feel inspired, or go to a seminar about a topic you are passionate about, and you can begin to feel alive again? Did you ever have a teacher at school that really believed in you, and who was always full of encouragement and could see your potential? Or maybe you had a parent who motivated you to achieve when you were a child? Those feelings of positivity and self-empowerment are crucial to success in business, and in life in general.

Having these positive experiences boosts you and helps create a life of self-belief and success. Likewise—if you were a child with a parent that constantly put you down, or you have a job that is boring and your boss couldn't care less about you, or you are easily replaced, or you find your friends are not really your friends, and they would make you the butt of the joke—these are all examples of how your self-worth can get crushed. Ideally, you have mastered self-belief, and you are not swayed by the situations you face, and you are a master of your emotions!

We both love the movie, *The Secret.* It is a powerful explanation of the law of attraction, and touches on all the different areas in life that can be affected. It is essential to success that you believe in yourself and your abilities, and your need to feel good about yourself. If you don't believe in yourself, the chances of you succeeding in property investing are slim. Imagine person A—let's call him Jim. Jim is hardworking but always doubts himself, and in fact, in his thoughts, he puts himself down, blaming his upbringing and his alcoholic father for never supporting him. Jim wallows in pity, and often second guesses himself about trying new things. Jim is unhappy, in a spiral of never ending uncertainty, and lives in the past, blaming other people for his misfortune. Take person B—let's call him Tom. Tom is also hardworking but often likes to try new things. He believes that if someone else can do something, then he can too. Although Tom also had an abusive alcoholic father, he takes responsibility for his own life, saying to himself, "I do not want to be that kind of negative influence on my own children." Tom is living in the present, and focuses on being able to change and try new things. Tom is happy and fulfilled in life, and strives for more. Everyone has a story; bad things happen to everyone; everyone has had issues in their lives—it's called *"so what."* It's how a person deals with it and gets on in their life that's the most important thing.

This last year has been transformational for us. We have come to realise the value and critical need of self-belief in our lives. *"Whether you think you can, or whether you think you can't, you are right either way." –* Henry Ford

Believing that you can do something, whether it's writing a book, like us, running a marathon, or building your own property portfolio, we believe that by having self-belief, that we can achieve the goal, and not only will it get us where we want to be, but it will get us there faster. We had been thinking about property investing for years. It was only by attending seminars, reading books, and speaking to mentors that gave us the self- belief that we could achieve our dreams—firstly, a life of financial freedom, and then to go further for abundant wealth. We are still on the road, enjoying this property journey, but now we wholeheartedly, 100%, believe in financial success.

Recently, we attended a seminar in London, UK, hosted by Darren Winters, from the Wealth Training Company. During his seminar, we were asked to think about our own beliefs about money. This is quite a good exercise, and we encourage you to think of ten beliefs that you think about money, or what was said to you about money when you were growing up. We will start you off with a couple that we had: 1) Money doesn't grow on trees. 2) We can't afford that. 3) The love of money is the route of all evil.

So, Darren gave us five of his wealth beliefs and challenged us to recite them until we really believed them. Nine months on, we continue to recite them, and we would challenge you, if you want to make a change, to do the same. It has made us feel so much more positive about money. It has opened our eyes to see all the wealth that surrounds us that is in the world. It keeps us open minded to receiving more wealth in life, including money.

Here are the 5 wealth beliefs that Darren gave us:

- I believe that if you are creative enough, you will find a way.
- I believe the more you give, the more you get.
- I believe that if someone else can do something, then so can I.
- I believe that the more I invest in myself and real education, the wealthier I become.
- I believe that anything is possible: if it's physically possible, it's possible.

Even if you don't have much self-belief to start, if you surround yourself with good people who are positive, who believe in themselves, and who can encourage you, then you will absorb this energy of self-belief. Then you, too, will be on your path to success. These daily affirmations are a fantastic tool to begin feeling courageous and motivated. There are plenty more affirmations that you could use, found on the internet, for other subjects. There are also meditation affirmations on YouTube that can start you off on the right foot for the day. It's amazing how a 10-minute affirmation session can wake you up, giving you energy for the rest of the day. There are longer ones—20 minutes, 30 minutes, or even an hour—however, we have found that 10 minutes is just enough to put us into a positive mindset. If you don't have enough time, and you are making excuses why you don't have the time, then why not get up earlier!?

Never Stop Learning

"Everything is a learning process; any time you fall over, it's teaching you to stand up the next time."
– Joel Edgerton

We find it interesting that at school we get taught information, and we learn different subjects and knowledge, taught by the teachers and peers; however, we are not taught HOW to learn. The way we learn as individuals can be very different to the next guy. There are a few different types of learning styles that you may or may not realise that are out there. They are:

Visual – The student will process information by looking at tables and graphs, or by pictures, or by watching a demo. These people tend to get fidgety when someone is purely just talking to them.

Audio – These students will retain more knowledge by reading, rereading, and then explaining the information themselves. Some students will find having background music helpful, while others will need complete silence to learn.

Doing – These students learn best by experimentation, touching, feeling, and a hands on approach to the learning. Often, these people find it difficult to keep still.

As you can see, there are different ways to learn rather than being talked to by a teacher. Even within the learning styles, there are several different types. This has just been a taster to show you that we are not all the same when it comes to learning, and you will need to find what works best for you. We think schools have come a long way to understanding these differences, but there is still a lot more that could be done. One size does not fit all. We were talking to a friend recently about Montessori schools. Montessori is a method of education where the approach to learning is centred round the child, and considers all aspects of the child as a whole: social, cognitive, emotional, and physical. This method was designed by Dr. Maria Montessori, and in our opinion, is an excellent way for the child to learn about what they are interested in, at a pace to suit themselves.

Never stop learning. The old can teach the young, but remember that the young can also teach the old, especially when it comes to technology, for example. It is important to have a willing heart when it comes to learning, and mistakes can teach us a lot about life, and especially not what to do for next time. If fact, mistakes are just one aspect of the learning process. When a child begins to start to walk, he doesn't give up the first time he falls over; he carries on until he can walk unassisted and freely on his own. It is the same with learning anything new. There will be times when you feel like giving up, or you might think that you are unable to master something, but with some persistence and time, it is amazing what you can achieve.

Even within our property development course with Development Discovery, we made sure to continually ask questions, and to question any areas or subjects that we didn't understand. Even though, sometimes, Jo has felt a little silly at asking a question, it was after the session that other partners on our course would come up to Jo and say, *"I'm glad you asked that, cos I didn't know either."* At the beginning of our property development course, we were given a number of large and complicated documents to read over and digest. Jo found this quite difficult, and it made her feel anxious. The way we got round this was in bite size segments, and Danny would read these aloud to Jo, and then she would write down any questions or points that were not understood. This really helped her get through the documents and overcome the problem, which gave her confidence that she could actually achieve. This gave her an immense boost.

I'm sure you would agree that our first 12 months as property investors have been like a rollercoaster ride. Buckle up, and sit tight as we race into the next chapter, where you will learn how to avoid some giant mistakes.

Chapter 9

Lessons Learned

Mistakes Are Good

"If no mistake you made, losing you are.
A different game you should play."
– Yoda

So, here is a lesson on what not to do. As we mentioned in Chapter 2, our biggest regret was buying a property that needed EVERYTHING doing to it, including a title split and paying for it in CASH! Yes, we thought it was a great deal, and that we would have a great profit at the end of it. But we were far too inexperienced to deal with this type of project. The first mistake we made was not keeping it simple. We should have bought a simple BTL property that needed a light refurbishment. The second mistake was to buy a property that needed a title split. Again, this is advanced stuff, and we were still learning the basics! The third mistake was hiring the builders that we did. Unfortunately, we have had a terrible experience with the builders. They were so slow, incompetent, and poorly managed by the project manager. A job that should have taken 3–4 months took nearly 7 months to complete.

We tied up all that cash by paying for the property outright! If we had known then what we know now, there is no way we would have bought that property. What would have been good was a book like this one, showing us the very basics, and how to stick to them to guarantee a steady flow of income from sound BTL properties!

"No matter how many mistakes you make or how slow you progress, you are still way ahead of everyone who isn't trying." – **Tony Robbins**

You may buy your property in the summer months, when the weather is dry and it's sunny, but bear in mind that when the rain comes, you may well have surprise leaks or roofing problems that you weren't aware of. If you notice a staining coming through the ceiling, it may indicate a leak from the roof area. If you can, go and investigate this. If you have a builder that you trust, they can give you a quote and deal with the problem before it becomes a nightmare. Generally, with a light refurbishment for BTLs, you should not need to replace the whole roof if there is a leak. It is recommended that you patch this up to keep the costs down. Wet patches penetrating a wall into your property will again be easily identified, as there will be staining or patches appearing. Sometimes just by feeling the wall from inside the property, you can feel the cold and the damp. It may be that there is water penetration into the wall due to poor pointing of the outside brickwork. Repointing is the process of renewing the pointing of render that is between each brick. Due to the exposure of the elements, this causes weathering to the masonry, and this allows water to come through. Don't shy away from this problem, as this is something that can easily be fixed. If it is left, it can become very costly, and you might even need to remove all of the interior wall plaster work to expose the problem. Ideally, steer clear from problems of this type of issue until you have some experience under your belt as a landlord. Try to find a sound property that needs a light refurbishment, with no structural changes.

Which? magazine carried out a survey of over 5000 customers. These were the top 5 complaints regarding builders:

Timing issues – One of the biggest complaints of builders is that they do not complete the project on time as agreed. This may be caused by poor weather conditions or lack of availability of the building crew due to being on another site. Within your builder's contract, you need to put a timing to how long the project will take to complete. If this timing is breached without reasonable explanation, then you will advise them that they are in breach of the contract, and that compensation can be claimed.

Work cost more than original quote – Get a number of quotes from builders, and ensure they are quoting like for like. Once you have decided on which builder you wish to use, you will need to get a contract written up. This contract can be essential if there are any disputes down the line. Getting an estimate from a builder is just that. It means that the price can vary, but it will give you a rough idea how much the works will cost. A quote, though, is generally the fixed price that you will pay. Never pay for any work upfront.

Poor quality job – If you are dissatisfied with the quality of work, it is important to let the builder know as soon as possible. Leaving any issues to the end can cause other knock on problems, and may cost the builder in time and other expenses to put this right. Generally, it is good practice to have staged payments. If something has gone wrong, then you have the choice to hold back the next staged payment until the issue is resolved.

Rubbish was left behind – Find out from your builder how they are going to dispose of the rubbish that will accumulate as a result of the works. Put this into the contract. Are they going to use a skip, and where will this be located? If it is to be placed on the street, you may need to obtain a local council permit.

Poor communication – Make sure that all channels of communication are open between you and your builder. It is important to be clear and concise with your communication. Preferably, any changes or requirements need to be put in writing, and this can then be confirmed by the builder to ensure a clear understanding. If you begin to have issues with communication (i.e. not answering your calls or emails), consider contacting the local trading standards.

Remember that unless you actually take action and try, you will never be successful. It is inevitable that you will make some mistakes along the way. But unlike in school, where we are taught that mistakes are wrong, and are told to *white out* words and rewrite them, or erase lines from a drawing, embrace mistakes and learn from them. The only mistake you can make is not to learn something from that experience. This is how we all learn, and you will see in time that the more of these property investments that you do, the more savvy you will become, and the less mistakes you will make.

When Things Go Wrong

"Success is not a destination, but the road that you're on. Being successful means that you're working hard and walking your walk every day. You can only live your dream by working hard towards it. That's living your dream."
– Marlon Wayans

Being a property investor can be a challenge, but this book will help you avoid the pitfalls when starting out. By staying positive and wide-eyed, it will help you to be able to identify the potential problems before they happen. If you keep focused on your goal, you will be able to achieve success. By getting educated now, and gaining an understanding of the downsides that can happen, will put you in a better position to choose the right properties for your portfolio. We've already mentioned that having people around you that are positive is essential, but you also need people who are prepared to work hard, and who you can trust.

When we purchased our property that we intended to title split, we were really excited when we got the keys. It was a property that another investor was selling. Two of the houses were habitable but needed new kitchens and bathrooms, and the walls needed painting to spruce it up. The basement apartment was just a shell, and needed everything done to it to make it rentable. Our initial builder had agreed that we would get weekly photos, and discussed a video walkthrough to show us progress. We had decided on a payment schedule, and being new to the industry and not wanting to cause any friction between us and the builder, we paid him upfront for materials for the initial stages of the project. In speaking to other property investors, now we have been advised that other than a small holding deposit to keep us within the builder's schedule, we should not pay money up front. If you are asked for a large sum of money up front, then this should be a *red flag*, and set off an alarm in your head. This should assist you to consider if you have chosen the right builder. If they are a professional builder, then they should have enough resources available to them to get through the first stage. They should have accounts with builder's merchants, which they are able to utilise to get materials. This will show that they are established, and this should give you confidence and trust. Once this project has started, and you can see the agreed progress has been made, then make sure that you pay your builder on time, and as agreed in your payment schedule.

On our project, we had agreed a total refurbishment time of 12 weeks. We had visited the site about 4 times during the build, but we started to have some doubts that we were on track when we got to about 8 weeks, and the houses were not finished, and the basement apartment had not much progress to show. The weekly photos stopped, and the video walkthroughs were not happening. The builder started to become more elusive, and we began to have difficulties in communicating, either via email or by phone calls or text. Our alarm bells began to ring, and so we planned an unannounced site visit. Upon arrival, instead of a team of builders working flat out, we found 2 guys, one of who was the site manager's uncle. We noticed that the monies that had been paid did not reflect what should have been completed, and that the project had virtually ground to a halt. With a heavy heart, but sensibly, we decided to get rid of the builders. We had held back only 5% of the agreed monies for the job, and the basement apartment still had mud walls, mud floors, and no kitchen or bathroom, and we had not seen any progress on what had been agreed in the contract. This gave us the problem of a *half-finished* job, and nearly all of the money allocated had been spent. We had allocated approximately 25% of our funds to complete the apartment with our original builder, and as this had not been achieved, we managed to agree by negotiation with him to receive some compensation. We used this to complete the 2 houses that had not been completed, and have land banked the apartment until a later stage.

Another issue we had with our original builder was with the apartment. The apartment is the actual basement of the 2 houses that we owned above, and needed a complete refurbishment. It has its own front door at street level to the rear of the houses, and we made arrangements with the local authority to register the property in its own entity, and have a separate address and postcode. We then got this property registered with Land Registry, UK. The apartment didn't actually have any separate utilities to it. We had to arrange to get water, gas, and electric installed into the premises. Water and gas actually did not cost us anything to get connected up to the street main, but electric was a different game. We applied to the appropriate company to get an electricity supply installed. We made the builder the point of contact with local contractors, and he was given the specification of how the channel needed to be dug, and what cladding needed to be in place to protect the main electric cable coming into the property. The builder was asked to take photos to prove that the ground had been correctly prepared. However, during our dispute, our builder filled in the channel dug for the electric main, and it transpired that he had not taken photographs; so the utility company refused to allow the main to be installed. For us to get electric installed, we would have to start the process again. This was very frustrating. Although these mistakes have been troublesome, we have learnt so much along the way and it is only through getting stuck in that you will learn and grow.

Spending Money

"You need to spend money to make money."
– Kam Dovedi

Being frugal when you are buying something can be and is often counterproductive. For example, have you ever bought a cheap mobile phone charger as a spare or replacement? Did it stand up to reasonable wear and tear? Probably not! I bet, after a while, it started to stop working properly, and maybe even became dangerous because bare threaded wires were exposed. Maybe in the end, you had to throw it away and buy another one. Hopefully, this time, you paid the premium and bought an authentic and original product that will now last you a reasonable about of time. So spending out can actually save you money, and in fact, going for the cheapest item on the shelf can actually cost you more money. Loss leaders are products that might appear to be cheap, but the peripherals for the product cost you a lot more. An example of this is buying a cheap printer. It is likely that the costs of the inks over a period of time will make the cheap printer very costly to run. So buying a more expensive printer, where there is more economy in the ink usage system, may be more advantageous over time.

With property, the same rule applies. If you take shortcuts in a purchase, then be prepared to have a cost at a later stage that you were not prepared for. If you buy a property for cash, and decide not to get a property valuation, you are virtually burying your head in the sand, and may be picking up a large bill to resolve any unidentified issues or risks. A valuation will give you some peace of mind that what you are paying is a reasonable price. It will also give you its estimated current market value. If you need a mortgage, the lender will commission a valuation. The valuation will give advice to the lender, as well as the property value and any issues or characteristics. This will include any concerns from the valuer due to building or land defects.

The valuation may identify dampness, subsidence, or any other structural condition, or even if Japanese knotweed is present (which may make the property unmortgageable). All of these issues may affect the value as security for the mortgage loan. The appraisal will also take into account recent sales prices of similar properties, location, and local amenities. A mortgage valuation is different from a property survey. The valuation will, as stated, check the valuation of the property, and if it is suitable for the lender to allow a mortgage. However, the property survey does not give a detailed inspection of the condition of the property. You may find, though, that a survey does give you a valuation. So check from the outset what report you are paying for, and what you are trying to achieve. The valuation is normally sent to the lender within 48 hours. Also, we had never heard of a *red book* valuation. If someone is referring to a valuation known as Red Book, then this is the name given to a valuation report, which complies with guidance from practitioners of the Royal Institution of Chartered Surveyor's Valuation Professional Standards.

Patching up a problem may fix the issue, but sometimes it is just masking the larger problem, and will end up costing you more. Your builder may have identified a damp wall. Your builder decides to make it look good for you so that you can get the property rented out. He paints over the problem wall area to give it a fresh look from any staining, but because he has not dealt with the problem by removing the paintwork and allowing the wall to dry out after a suitable treatment, the problem returns. Imagine the inconvenience and how the tenant will feel if another builder needs to come in and rectify the problem. It may even mean that the property is uninhabitable, and you need to rehouse the occupants for a short period of time. This will be at your cost, and you may not be able to get any compensation from your building insurance. You may have identified that a double glazed window seems to have water penetration or misting inside the glass. This may indicate that the neoprene window gasket or seals have deteriorated or failed, and warm air has gotten in between the glass. Your builder may decide to ignore this problem, but it is probably better to replace the window before the property is tenanted, as again, there will be inconvenience to the tenants once the property is occupied.

Your accountant is an integral part of the *power team*. Having a good accountant who understands property tax is essential. So going for a general accountant who will invariably be cheaper may actually cost you more money, because they will be unaware of certain tax savings that you are eligible for.

We would suggest that employing a builder who gives the cheapest quote may not necessarily be a good idea in the long run. You will probably find numerous hidden costs, and end up paying more to get these issues resolved.

Choose Your Friends Wisely

"The key is to keep company only with people who uplift you, whose presence calls forth your best."
– Epictetus

If we said to you that in five years' time you could precisely predict where you will be—what you will be doing at work, what your income will be, or what direction your life will take—you may be thinking, "This is impossible; how can anyone predict this?" Well, the answer is actually very easy: it's the people that we have around us. Our life's direction is massively influenced by the people that we mix with. We have friends that are not on our wavelength. It has been a difficult decision to make, but we have had to end some friendships that we have had, because they are toxic. Some of the people that we have left behind are even family members. You can't choose your family, and you may think you are stuck with them whether you like it or not, but we disagree. Life after getting rid of certain people is better on so many levels. Some of the people we have said goodbye to have not really cared for us in the way we deserve. We believe that we should be treated with respect, as we treat others with respect. Some of these people were such a drain on us. They would continually talk about the terrible past events that occurred, or their continuous problems with their health or work environment. One friend we said goodbye to recently used to talk about herself nonstop, and we used to play a game to see if she would ask us how *we* were doing. She rarely asked us! We became an agony aunt and uncle, and an unpaid one at that!

You will no doubt have heard the phrase, *"You are the sum of the 5 people you spend your most time with."* Now, although we don't think this applies to your own kids, we do believe that your family members and friends play a big part on how you get on in life. If you want more wealth, then hang out with wealthier people than yourself. If you want to be smarter, then you will need to hang out with people who are smarter than you. If you want to moan and have negative thoughts, then spend time with negative people who moan all the time. Is there anyone in your life that sticks out to you that you need to say goodbye to? In fact, you may not want to be that drastic and cut them off completely. Consider distancing yourself from them. Spend less time with them; don't always answer the phone to them. Don't always reply to their texts. Remember, they gain something from you, by you listening to them moan or complain constantly. We have been brought up to not interrupt people or challenge people if they are talking, and to be a good listener by listening to people's problems. But there comes a time when you need to take stock of how much time is being wasted listening to people's complaints. The issues can have a negative effect on your own emotions. We all know those types of people who have sour puss faces when they are older, who clearly complained for most of their lives about one thing or another. And then you have those other people whose wrinkles are beautiful when they smile, as it shows a history of thankfulness, gratefulness, love, and success. They will often have a glint in their eyes that encapsulates the positive energy that they give off.

Take a moment here to close your eyes for 30 seconds, and think about some people who really make you feel positive, and that you would want to spend more time with. We also consider listening to people's books on www.audible.com. If we want to hang out with Bob Proctor, for example, we listen to his audio books, or go to his conferences, or take up his mentorship programme, and listen or watch some of his YouTube videos. This way, his ideas, his teaching, his way of positive thinking, will rub off on us. To put this into another perspective, what do you do when your computer gets a virus? If you don't deal with it, then it will slow down your system. If you leave it on your computer, the virus may even corrupt or even destroy your computer, and you will have no safe data. The solution seems obvious: you need to purge the virus from your computer by using some antivirus software. Nagging, negative harmful people will have a destructive impact on your life. As with your computer, if you eliminate the virus, then your computer will work more efficiently; and with your life, without these negative people around you, you will function in a better, more effective and smarter way.

We appreciate that to actually do this and to *delete* people from your life may be very hard. But your life will be transformed. Undoubtedly, and initially, you may think that you have made the wrong decision, but give yourself time. After a short while, you will see the difference, and then you will notice how your days—then your weeks, and then longer—feel so much better. Now that you know what caused you this negativity, and you have purged this out of your life, you can go out there and get friends that will surround you with their positivity. The time that you had been spending on worrying and stressing, you can now nurture into achieving positive outcomes. In the future, you will be able to look back at why you put up with those viruses on your computer. We all know that a computer runs better without a virus, and similarly, your life will run better as well. Spend time with property investors who have achieved much more than you already—people who are positive, goal orientated, and who can help you achieve your goals.

"Associate yourself with people of good quality, for it is better to be alone than in bad company." – Booker T Washington

Teamwork is Essential

"Unity is strength… when there is teamwork and wonderful collaboration, wonderful things can be achieved."
– Mattie Stepanek

It has been ideal working together as husband and wife on our property investing business. We work really well together, and our strengths and weaknesses complement each other. We are grateful that we are able to get on so well and accept each other's flaws, and continually encourage each other to learn and grow as we develop our relationship. So, too, does our business relationship grow. There are several husband and wife teams that work well, including Robert and Kim Kiyosaki, and Grant and Elena Cardone. You don't need to be married for this to work. Take Rob Moore and Mark Homer, for example. In fact, a brilliant partnership—they met at a networking event. Rob had the time, and Mark had the money, and together they have built their empire. Relationships take time. Even in business, it can take months or years to develop trust and commitment. Finding people who you click with is key to team work; although in saying that, it is not people who are just like you that you want on your team. In fact, the less like you that they are, the better, as they will have different opinions and skills to offer.

So what characteristics make up a good team? It is imperative that a team is able to communicate with each other. During challenging times, it is essential to have open communication channels. The last thing you want is for a team member to feel so overwhelmed or angry, and then shut themselves off and not respond to emails, or answer their phone or respond to messages. There will be occasions when your differing perspectives make you want to stand your ground on an issue, but be prepared to listen, to understand, and to be adaptable to the other person. Having team players who have vision and can stay focused on the goal will allow you to keep your business running smoothly. Being committed to the cause is essential. Without this, there will be no drive or enthusiasm for the business, and your business will ultimately fail. Having trust in your team members is vital. If you are unable to leave your partners to make certain decisions, then the stress and the worry of a particular role will pass over to you, and that is not good for anyone. Encourage each other to succeed, and even the small successes should be celebrated. Make sure you have some *downtime* to allow you to have a break from the stresses of the day-to-day property business.

We are delighted to have found an amazing property team who we have joined forces with, and we are able to learn as we leverage their vast experience, knowledge, and connections. Working with our partners from Development Discovery (DD), the senior team brings a wealth of experience in property development.

Alan Christie – Alan heads up the internal development team. He has a vast experience of property development, since the early 1990s. He has worked on both small and large development projects, ranging from small, twelve-home rural communities, up to housing estates of seventy-five homes. He has seen firsthand the property cycles, and the economic effects of a global financial crisis. One of Alan's strengths is dealing and communicating with people, and especially managing construction teams.

Eduardo Prato – Eduardo is the team systems guy. In 2004, he started his property business, and now has his own property letting agency. His background as a navy helicopter pilot instructor and examiner brings this discipline, and organisation skills, to this fantastic company.

Pauline Heron – Pauline is the business psychologist of the company. It was in the early 1990s that Pauline began to actively invest in property, and now owns a successful letting agency in multiple locations across the Midlands, UK. After a twenty-five-year military career, and creating a number of businesses alongside, she has begun to focus in a variety of sectors as a business psychologist. Pauline brings great understanding and creative entrepreneurial ideas to the Development Discovery team.

Aidan Heron – Aidan is the technical head guy in DD. Being Pauline's son, he was brought up in the property industry, and was able to learn as he grew up. Since graduating from university in physics, he has set up his own property business, with a focus on high yields. Introverted in nature, he could spend all day in front of the computer, quite happily. Any technical or geeky questions, then Aidan is the go-to guy.

Charles Zhao – Charles is the finance guy. After graduating with a 1st class honours in Economics from the University of Cambridge, Charles has specialised in risk and finance by assisting top tier UK banks (including HSBC, Barclays and Lloyds) in setting up post crisis risk management systems.

You can contact us at www.phillipsrealestate.co.uk/contact if you would like to talk through joining this fantastic team and becoming a partner yourself.

Being an entrepreneur is not all about working on your own. Grant Cardone would call this a *solopreneur*. *"Coming together is a beginning; staying together is progress; and working together is success."* – Henry Ford

Personality Types

"The art of delegation is one of the key skills
any entrepreneur must master."
– Richard Branson

Danny is quite an extrovert. He enjoys speaking to people, interacting, and communicating. He finds that doing these things will recharge his batteries. Jo finds the opposite to be true, and although she enjoys speaking to people too, she finds that she can get quite drained, quite easily, and likes her alone time to recharge.

It is good to find out your personality type in order to have a better understanding of who you are and what you can bring to the table. We have both done a Myers Briggs personality test years ago, and had a general understanding. The online personality test is based on the personality type theory, by Isabel Briggs Myers and Carl Jung.

There are 16 personality types. We took the test recently to see if our personality type had changed over the years. We found that our results were exactly the same, even though we felt some of our answers had changed, and we were answering differently.

If you want to take the test, go to www.mbtionline.com. There are 93 questions to answer, and it will take you about 15 minutes to go through. Your result will tell you what your *type* is, and it will give you 4 letter indicators, which describe your personality. These are where you focus your attention.

Extraversion (E) or Introversion (I) The way you take in information – Sensing (S) or INtuition (N) How you make decisions – Thinking (T) or Feeling (F) How you deal with the world – Judging (J) or Perceiving (P)

Danny's personality test result shows that he is ENTJ, so his attention is focused on Extraverted, iNtuitive, Thinking, and Judging. Jo's personality test shows that she is INFJ, so her attention is focused on Introversion, iNtuition, Feeling, and Judging.

"It is up to each person to recognize his or her true preferences." – Isabel Briggs Myers

Through our Development Discovery partners, we were invited to join them on a Wealth Dynamics course, created by Roger James Hamilton. We had a full day of training after having taken the test, and were then able to identify which of the 8 wealth profiles was our natural path. These are the 8 wealth profiles. Your profile will be made up of a percentage of some of the following: *Mechanic, Creator, Star, Lord, Supporter, Accumulator, Trader, and Deal Maker.*

There is great value in both tests. The Myers Briggs test tells you more about your personality, and the Wealth Dynamics test gives you a clearer direction in your career and on which pathway to follow in your job and business. Different personalities compliment other people. It's about working together as a team, and utilising each of your strengths and weaknesses to achieve your goals to combat your weaknesses.

"Focus on your strengths, not your weaknesses, and follow your flow."
– Roger Hamilton

When you complete the test, your profile will give you the confidence to spend time and focus on the things that you love, and the courage to say no to things or people that don't bring out the best in you. You will find that your stress levels will plummet, while your sense of fulfilment will rocket. Everybody has a different set of tools and gifts that make up your natural personality. If you fight against your natural rhythm, life will be a struggle. We have found that by doing this test, it has made us realise that there are many different ways that people think about things, how they respond, and how they take action. By effectively utilising your tools, you will be able to make a difference in the world.

There are tasks out there that you don't want to do, which other people love to do.

You may hate doing all of the research and analytics, but your strength might be speaking to people and engaging new conversations.

You might shy away from public speaking, but others may thrive in, and thoroughly enjoy, that environment.

Maybe when you know that you need to negotiate on an issue, you shrink away, shudder, and draw away from the problem.

When the time has come and you need to make an offer to the vendor or estate agent, and you feel that this is not something that you are able to do.

There is no wrong or right; embrace who you are, and live to fight another day. Once you have your project, identify all of the tasks that need to be completed, and then be mindful of what you are good at doing and what you would prefer to leverage out.

Now that you have identified your skills and strengths, we can jump right into the very last chapter of this book, where you will find how to create your ultimate success, and how to achieve the life that you want.

Chapter 10

Living the Dream

Achieving Financial Freedom

*"If you are born poor, it is not your mistake,
but if you die poor, then it is your mistake."*
– Bill Gates

Knowing that while you are on holiday, relaxing by the beach, money is coming into your bank account, and you don't have to do anything to work for it, is a wonderful feeling. Having enough money coming in every month to cover all your living expenses, including some fun stuff and holidays, is a dream. Knowing that you do not *have* to have a job ever again will give you the freedom and choices to do whatever you want in life. By investing in property, you can make this happen!

By making money work for you, in an investment, rather than having to work yourself into the ground by working 40/50/60+ hours each week, *for* money, is financial freedom. Once you have money coming in from renting out your BTL property or properties, you will soon be able to give up your full time job, but only if you want to. You may like your job and choose to continue working, but that will still be your *choice* rather than a necessity. Having the choice then becomes liberating. Once you have surplus money coming in on a regular basis, it gives you the freedom to spend your time however you like. You may want to spend more time with family, or traveling to places that you had only dreamed of, or buy that dream car. Or maybe it will inspire you to work even harder. The key here is to stop working for money, and to get your money working for you. Jo's parents recently got solar panels fitted to the roof of their house. Whilst on a recent holiday with them, Jo's mum remarked how wonderful it was to know that whilst she was on holiday, the sun was shining back home and making money for them. It is the exact same thing when it comes to an investment property. One of the biggest parts of having financial freedom is having a life without fear and worry about money, and what may happen in the future if you didn't have enough. Many people in their 60s and 70s are having to continue working because they are not financially free, and cannot have the lifestyle they are accustomed to unless they continue to work for money. We don't know about you, but we do not like the idea of that! In days gone by, people used to work for a company for 30 years or so, and then receive a nice pension at the end of it, for retirement. These days, people do not tend to stay in a job for life, and the pension schemes are tight and may not give you the money that will be required to live a comfortable retirement.

By investing some time and effort, and money upfront in an investment BTL property, you will be able to get a regular passive income—your very own ATM—and overtime, that property is more than likely to go up in value, giving you the increase in equity too. Remember that your debt on the property will in a sense be going down, even if it is not a repayment type of mortgage, because inflation will make the debt easier to pay in the future. It is a win-win situation. It is a beautiful thing when you realise this. No matter what age you are when this bombshell of a penny drops, you will be able to take steps to change your life, and create cash flow, along the way to financial freedom. In essence, financial freedom is when you can live comfortably from passive income that you do not have to work for. The key here is to create multiple pillars of passive income.

Imagine a table, for example. You know that if it had only 1 leg that it would soon and easily fall over. With 3 legs, there would be a greater stability, and by having 4 legs, the table becomes stable. The same is true in regard to your investments. It is all very well having 1 BTL, but what if something happened to that investment that made living there impossible for your tenants!? Your passive income stream suddenly dries up, and you are left with a liability on your hands. If, however, you had different sources of income, from other properties, then you are reducing your risk and making yourself, your business, and your life more financially stable. If you can set up systems in your life, where you have multiple streams of passive income, you will attract financial freedom, just as a magnet attracts metal. You can have anything, be anything, and do what you want in life. If you can hold it in your mind, it can become a reality. It might not always work out exactly as you planned, but now you know you will be able to look back and see in your life how this law of attraction has been working so far. Thoughts become things. If you think about debt, and worry about debt, then all you are going to get is more debt. If you think about financial abundance, then you will attract the people and be able to go to places where you can begin to learn more about financial abundance, and bring it into your life.

Have you ever heard of the 80/20 rule? It originates from 1895, when Vilfredo Pareto founded the Pareto Principle. This principle can be applied to life and time in any circumstance. In Timothy Ferriss's book, *The Four-Hour Work Week*, he endorses the 80/20 principle. The theory behind this is that 80% of your important output is produced from 20% of your time. If you choose to redirect your attention, and pinpoint those tasks that create the best output, then you will be able to increase your productivity in life exponentially. It is this principle that the whole book centres itself on. It is for that reason that the book is called *The Four-Hour Work Week*. This mantra is basically all about prioritising and only doing the 20% that is important in your life, and ignoring the other 80%. If you want to learn more about his interpretation of the principle, then go ahead and read the book.

By reviewing how you spend your time every day, you will be able to clearly see how much time you are spending on IGTs—income generated tasks—and by increasing the time spent doing IGTs, your income will increase. To analyse how you spend your days, read *Start Now, Get Perfect Later*, by Rob Moore. The great thing about this book is that it is written by Rob, who is an expert at property investing, and always includes his interpretation through the eyes of a highly experienced property investor.

Multiple Streams of Passive Property Income

"You have brains in your head. You have feet in your shoes. You can steer yourself any direction you choose."
– Dr. Seuss

Once you have reached your dream of financial freedom, you will no longer need to be working in a JOB. You will not need to work hard for money, as all your expenses are being paid off by your investment income. You may already have a few single BTLs up your sleeve, and be ready for your next challenge. So now what!? Many people confuse the concept of multiple streams of income with getting several part-time jobs. This is far from ideal, because you will be trading your time for money and, eventually, run out of time! Well, this is the perfect time to start looking into other property strategies. By choosing another way to create a passive income, you will be making money while you sleep. It is best to get a good overview of the different types of property investments that are out there for you. There are several different property strategies that you might be interested in looking at. At this stage, you will need to consider carefully your next steps. Be sure to consider the contacts that you have already made, who you are networking with, and what information you already have under your belt that can assist you in your next venture.

HMOs are great because the yields tend to be a lot higher than the single BTLs. However, HMOs tend to have a high occupancy turnover rate and, therefore, often have higher letting fee costs. A lot of agencies tend to charge a higher maintenance fee in order to have a compensation for the more frequent issues and problems that arise by having multiple occupants under one roof. Try to imagine who might live in a HMO. It could be a university town, and only a 10-minute walk to the university! A perfect location! You will need to be prepared for the fact that students may have parties, and things will get spilled or broken, and these items will need replacing. There can be problems with HMOs due to the fact that people don't always know each other and may not get on. It is best to find a specialist HMO letting agency that has experience and deals with HMOs on a daily basis. You might prefer the idea of making some money from a title split of a property, and then renting or selling off each property. You will need to consider the length of time that it will take to convert a property and to calculate the costs involved in the refurbishment, and do all the same due diligence as you have on your BTL. There will be additional legal fees to be covered for splitting a title and, of course, you will need to get planning permission from your local authority. It's always wise to consider the end goal when you do this, as you may find that the figures don't work as a rental, and it might be worth leaving well alone.

Commercial conversions are particularly popular at the moment in the UK. Due to the housing shortage, councils appear to be more lenient in agreeing to a change of use of a property during the planning process. Consider holiday lets as a passive income. Here, you can rent the property out on a short-term basis, to holiday makers. Be aware that although there is a good profit to be made during the high seasons, the low seasons can leave the income stream a little dry. You will need to calculate all the costs for the area, as you may find a sweet spot where you are happy with all the income from the seasons, as it evens out. There may be high marketing costs to be considered, depending on the demand in the area. With short-term holiday lets, there will be a high frequency turnover, and additional cleaning costs may rise.

Rent to rent has become more popular than ever. This strategy is for the creatives amongst us that can see the potential of a property. The idea is that you rent the property off the landlord for a fixed period of time, potentially at a lower rate in return for a long term, and then you find tenants to rent it from you. You will need to be completely upfront with the landlord in this situation, but they are often delighted to get a guaranteed rental income. By doing this, you could consider turning the property into serviced accommodation, and rent the rooms out individually. This way, you will be able to pocket the difference after costs. It's a great way of making money without having to pay down a large deposit.

Rent to rent is a brilliant way to make money quickly if you can find the right property to rent. The downside is that although you are essentially skimming the cream off the top of the milk, there is not usually enough money left over to get a management agency to look after the property so it tends to be a hands on investment. Be mindful that this approach does not give you an asset, you are not in control of the property, and the owner may decide to sell in the future. Lease options are similar to *rent to rent*, but it gives the buyer the *option* to purchase the property in the future, for a fixed amount, if they decide to. By creating a lease option, you, the buyer, will be taking on the responsibilities and obligations of the owner, and renting it out. Lease options are not as popular currently as they once were in a recession, where landlords were trying to wash their hands of some of their properties and responsibilities, but there are still opportunities to be had.

It is best to choose one property strategy and focus on it before starting on another one. Whichever strategy you choose, be sure to go over this book again, and remember to get a mentor. Having a mentor is the surest and fastest way to learn everything there is to know about your next steps, from someone who you trust. They will give you correct impartial advice, and they will also tell you honestly if they do not agree with your direction.

Persistence is a Virtue

"The chief cause of unhappiness is trading what you want most for what you want right now."
– **Zig Ziglar**

Having and setting goals definitely is a motivator for us. One of the ways that we've brought this to a visual reality is to have a goals board. We went to Hobbycraft, bought a massive piece of card, and then we went through magazines and the internet. We printed off pictures of goals and dreams, and stuck them onto our piece of card. This is our vision board, and we tend to keep it in the living room where we get to see it the most. It helps us to visualise these joint goals and dreams, every day, and reinforces and reiterates what we want for our future.

Also consider less materialistic goals; for example, supporting a charity that you believe in. Maybe you can start up a business that will help and support a large number of people. It is more difficult to find cut-out and stick-on goals for your relationships and children. Maybe you could find a saying or a phrase that sums up the thoughts you have, and stick that on your board instead. Having a vision board is a great way to motivate yourself to keep going. Everyone has bad days, but it is how you react to them and how quickly you stand up again that will define you as a person. Property is an asset class that will give you the freedom to have more choices in life. It's as simple as that. Knowing your reason—your *why*—for wanting the financial freedom, will be the thing that can ground you, and can help you to keep going when times are tough. It is easy to go along to network meetings and see everyone being happy, and to think that everyone else has got themselves together and that they know what they are doing. The truth is, just like on Facebook, people tend to put on a brave face and show what is going well. People do not tend to highlight the bad bits of their life, as people like to keep up their appearances. Once you get to know these people better, you will soon realise that they have concerns and problems, just like you. Everyone does! The key is to figure out quickly how to fix it, or how to get someone else to fix it for you. It doesn't matter how much money you have; it's not money that will fix the problem. Rich people still have problems, so don't be disillusioned.

So, we ask again, what's stopping you from having your dreams and making your dreams come true? If it's purely money, then carry on reading, and we'll tell you our story of how we have become closer to fulfilling our dreams and making them a reality in our lives. If you are not doing property investing full time, then by allocating yourself a time that you can focus on property related matters will really assist you in achieving your goal. You will then have a dedicated time to stop everything else in your life for this priority. During this time, turn off your phone, or if you can't bear to do that, activate a *Do Not Disturb*, or something similar. Stop all ringing, buzzing, and vibrating notifications, to give yourself 100% *no-distraction* time.

We have gone through different phases during our property journey so far. Through difficult times, we have asked ourselves why we are doing this. We have had some soul searching through these difficult times, but we have always come out on top. We can understand why people give up. But we are not going to. We are in this for the long run. We have the property *bug*, and this is pushing us to continue to learn more and more, and to find creative ways in getting finances in place to get the next property, with the aim of doing it again and again and again. Living together, enables us to bounce off each other and pull the other up when they are down. If you are on this journey as an individual, it is best to have someone who can encourage you to carry on through these difficult times; someone who you can call up whenever you are in times of need, but also someone who you can confide in, who can guide you and inspire you. Make yourself accountable to this person by agreeing to make contact with them; for example, every week, to give them an update of your progress. We do this with our mentor, Kam Dovedi, by sending him a Friday text. Alternatively, you could find an accountability partner who is also in the property industry. You can then ask each other questions, and you can talk about your progress. This partner will motivate you, and this will hopefully be sufficient to keep you moving forward towards your property goals.

The way that we have motivated ourselves has been to listen to audio books that encourage us to keep focused and not get discouraged. We found Bob Proctor's book, *7 Power Principles for Success*, to help us to stay focused, encouraged, and enthused. Another way to refresh our energy is by going to networking events and being surrounded by likeminded people. At these events, we have been motivated and rejuvenated.

Dreams Are the Seedlings of Reality

"Anyone who lives within their means suffers
from a lack of imagination."
– Oscar Wilde

What are your aspirations? What are your dreams and hopes for your future? We have a goal that we are purposely and consciously working towards. We have an ambition in mind, and we are both dedicated to invest our energy, resources, and time into achieving this goal. We are also prepared to cut back on other temptations that may give us a short-term win but are not meeting our long-term goal, which is the bigger picture.

Take a look around where you are sitting. Maybe you are sitting at home reading. You are surrounded by all the things in your life that were once a thought in your head. You had decided to buy that sofa, and you chose the colour and the style. First, you had to think about it with your mind, and now, here it is in your life. Consider this for a moment: it's the same with every single thing in your life. Hopefully, you will be getting the idea of how your thoughts can become things, and how you create your own life and circumstances. Things don't just happen for no reason at all. There is always a catalyst, and you will see where it started if you look far enough back. The more creative you are, and the more that you can imagine, the more your desires and dreams will become a reality. Somewhere from preschool to early 20s, we are discouraged from dreaming and thinking big. It is usually by people who dreamt big once but nothing came of it, or maybe that person got burnt along the way and doesn't want you to get hurt also. Do you think Elon Musk and Richard Branson don't dream big? Of course, they do! That is why they are doing what they are doing!

There is something in us that aches when we see an adult telling a child to be more realistic in life. Jo volunteers at a local school and helps out during arts and crafts lessons. Recently, she had a young girl of about 6 tell her that she wanted to be a pop star. Jo didn't crush her dreams by saying that it is highly unlikely that she would achieve this kind of success, and to consider thinking about a more realist retail job in a department store, for example; but Jo encouraged her by saying, *"Why not? That is a great idea! If somebody else can do it, then why not you?"* The girl was delighted with the encouragement, and proceeded to sing her heart out. We really do believe that if you follow your dreams, you will achieve them. By taking responsibility for your circumstances, you can take the reins of your own life and create whatever you like. We are not destined to be at the discretion of our own habits, unless we choose to be! By looking at what you can learn from a situation, rather than moaning and complaining about it, you can change it for the better. The more that we practice this way of thinking, the more in control we feel, and the more excited it makes us feel, because suddenly, a world of untold possibilities opens up.

It is the same with limiting beliefs. We all have them; it's just that some of us have a lot more than others. We develop our beliefs in childhood, and they get reinforced as life goes on. Unless you are aware of what your limiting beliefs are, then you will be destined to live a life that has been holding you back. If you are ready for more, to have more, to do more, and to expect more out of life, then think what your beliefs are, write them down, examine them, and consider them. If they limit you in some way, then you will need to replace them with a different belief. It is not easy to just say, *"That's it; I am not thinking like that anymore."* No, it is better to reframe your belief, and replace it with a different beat to the drum. You may need to write it out and look at it frequently. It can help to read it out loud and let it absorb in until it is your *go-to phrase.* You will soon find, by mixing with other property investors, and other wealthy people, that the rich think in a different way.

Steve Jobs had a massive dream during his lifetime, and he was certainly revolutionary in his time. He died on 5th October 2011. He was the co-founder of Apple Computers. Steve had an inspiration in how we embrace technology and how we consume information, and even after his death, his legacy lives on. It is likely that his inspiration has influenced your life or people around you.

Insights into Phillips Real Estate

"The future belongs to those who believe
in the beauty of their dreams."
– Eleanor Roosevelt

So, to date, we have a small portfolio of BTLs in Greater Manchester, England. They are tenanted and are bringing in monthly rental. It is a wonderful feeling each month when that money lands in your bank account. We employ the services of a property management company to deal with the day-to-day issues that may arise. We don't want to get that call at 2am in the morning from a distressed tenant. It is problems, such as a leaky toilet or a tap that won't turn off, or a boiler that won't give out any hot water, and so showering and central heating systems have failed, that we didn't want to have to worry about.

For the services of the property management company, we pay a percentage of our monthly rental income, and for that, they deal with everything; for example: taking professional photos of our properties so that they could promote and advertise our houses on the internet, to prospective tenants; vetting tenants to ensure the applicant/s were legitimate and had sufficient funds to pay the monthly rental; maintenance and repair issues; taking deposits and securing sureties; assuring that short hold tenancy agreements were signed; gas and electrical safety certificates, and Energy Performance Certificate (EPC), were given to the tenant; full property inventory; pursing evictions if required.

For us, it is about leveraging our time and using someone else's expertise and knowledge on landlord-tenant law.

A current project we are doing is a commercial to residential HMO deal, and it is currently going through planning. We are loving the new direction and learning about property development. Now, that is a whole new book in itself!

Having worked alongside Development Discovery here in the UK over the last year, and having completed their HMO course that they offered, we have decided to join forces with a large group of people, also on the Development Discovery property development course, in order to learn the process, from planning through to sales, of building new homes. We recently had our mastermind week, which was in the south of France, and we learnt all about the deal that they are currently looking at. It is a fantastic project, which involves building a housing estate. Why build one house when you can build 100! Knowing that the Development Discovery team has years and years of experience in property development, and in the property sector, we felt confident that we would like to invest as an equity share partner in the deal.

During the mastermind week we stayed at an amazing villa in the hills of Nice, which was stunning. It was such a beautiful place, with six separate apartments, a huge kitchen, and another outside kitchen, with gardens, a pool, and tennis courts! In this relaxed, luxurious atmosphere, we were easily able get to know the other partners involved in the project. Every morning, we would gather and sit around a giant, long table, and eat croissants and yummy French breakfast stuff, and drink coffee. Shortly after, we would get stuck into learning, for the rest of the morning. It was a very steep learning curve for us, as we did not know as much as others in the group. But saying that, we were by no means the least knowledgeable. Alan Christie gave a detailed overview of the project and the different teams and responsibilities involved. We are in the group that deals with the Reserve Matters, and also another team that specifically deals with the marketing of the project. There are about 4 people in each team, and each partner gets to be in two groups so they can really learn the ins and outs of what is needed. We are all responsible for our contributions to the appraisals and funding. After a wonderful lunch, we would get back to work, and learnt more about the development process.

The Development Discovery team is always encouraging us to ask questions, and between us, we had a lot! It was great to hear others asking questions that we had not considered. It definitely sped up our learning by doing this. The evenings were free for us to do as we pleased. One evening, we all went out to a restaurant nearby, and took over nearly half the restaurant! It was a wonderful atmosphere, and a great way to get to know the other partners in the team.

During our week's stay in Nice, we went on a tour of Monaco, around the Monte Carlo race course, and took in the inspiring scenery and the lush apartments and hotels that there were on offer. The yachts in the harbour were just so beautiful, and we really saw the opulent lifestyle that money can buy, and how money is not an issue for so many people. This was also a great aspiration to us, and we found it completely inspiring. It is easy to sit at home worrying about bills or debt, but when you visit places like this, it really encourages you to stay positive and on track. Property developing is a long-term strategy. From start to finish, it can take years, not months. This housing estate project is likely to take 3–4 years to complete; however, we really feel that we will learn so much along the way that the time aspect becomes not quite so important. At the end of the project, and when all the houses are sold, the profits will be divided and shared. The idea is that we will start a new project every year, so in 4-years' time, we will have 4 development projects on the go, and we will be getting a capital sum every year. When we do, we intend to invest it back into our own portfolio, buying more BTL properties but also reinvesting into Development Discovery, creating a funding cycle. We are really excited about this project and are looking forward to really getting stuck in.

Take Action Now

"The best way to predict the future is to create it."
– Abraham Lincoln

The purpose of this book is to give you, the reader, a 12-month crash course, without taking any financial risk and buying your first investment property. We want you to have an understanding of what the property industry can give you, and what you can get out of it. We hope that our stories and guidance can help you buy your very first property investment, safe in the knowledge that you have done your due diligence. So, what does the future hold for you? Do you have a dream yet? Or do you still have that little voice inside your head telling you that you can't do this, or that you can't afford it? Hopefully, we have shown you ways to combat that little voice in your head, and you can put him/her to the back of your mind as you press on towards your goal.

It is helpful to write a journal to record the progress of your journey. You will find this helpful to be able to look back on and see how far you have come. It is all too easy to forget your pathway, and so recording your highs and your lows will allow you to reflect, to get a deeper understanding, and to make changes accordingly. This is something that is personal to you, and you can put your thoughts, emotions, and frustrations down. With the simplicity of technology, you don't even have to actually write it down. You can speak it into your computer, and it will type it for you. We used this option when first writing our book. Unfortunately, sometimes spelling was not the best. But don't be a perfectionist; reading it back later will probably make you laugh. Maybe rereading the book now, while it is fresh in your mind, is a good option here. The second time you read things, other thoughts and more understanding will be there. You may wish to make notes this second time, if you haven't done so already.

We have three main lessons that we would like you to take away from this book:

Don't act on emotions – You may have come across what looks like the perfect property to buy as your first buy to let. It is in the right location, has great views, and is surrounded by local amenities, but the figures don't work. However, no matter how many times you calculate it, the yield is too poor. You need to trust the figures. Do your due diligence. This is key and will save you time and money in the future. Don't underestimate it. By calmly walking away from a deal, and taking the time to do your investigations, it will give you the breathing space you require in order to assess your emotions.

Good education is vital – Be prepared for some study, and don't expect to have great deals fall into your lap without first educating yourself. It is best to invest some money into good education when you first start out. This will set you up for your future as a property investor. We have mentioned some fantastic property educational companies that run extensive courses and provide webinars—such as Development Discovery, Progressive Property, and Premier Property— and this is where you can meet likeminded people on the same property path as you. We suggest that you get stuck in, and attend as many of these meetings as you can. By attending these meetings or courses, you will begin to have your mind opened to ideas that you hadn't even considered. *You don't know what you don't know.* There is always something new to learn, and at these network events or mastermind days, you will have the opportunity to listen and to speak to experts in the field about a variety of subjects that can help you with your personal property development.

Learn from your mistakes—fast – It is horrible to make a mistake, and it can be even worse if you have got a big price tag attached to it. But making mistakes is a natural process in life. It is easy to beat yourself up and to think that it's all gone wrong and want to give up, but if you can step outside of the problem, and look at the wider picture, then you will learn faster not to make the same mistake again. You will find valuable lessons to light your way as you go forward. You can waste time wallowing, going over and over things, but the best thing is to stand tall, accept that you have made the mistake, and be prepared to move forward.

We reiterate that we are not experts, even though we have learnt loads this last year. We felt compelled to write this overview, as there were no other books in the market that expressed the whirlwind adventure that you can expect from jumping into the property investing world. If you have been putting off investing for one reason or another, then we would encourage you to take action now, and to begin your property education before you buy your first buy to let (BTL). The longer you put it off, the longer it will take to get that passive income. So, find a mentor, sign up to a course or webinar, and continue reading. Why not read some of the books we have suggested? You can find a list for your convenience at the end of this book.

We wish you all the best and every success on your own adventure, and maybe, one day, we can meet, and you can tell us your own twelve-month journey. Be sure to share your learning with your friends and family so that they, too, can enjoy financial freedom and success.

Books that we recommend, in no particular order:

Think and Grow Rich, Napoleon Hill
The 7 Power Principles for Success, Bob Proctor
Start Now, Get Perfect Later, Rob Moore
The Secret, Rhonda Byrne
The Richest Man in Babylon, George S. Clason
Money, Rob Moore
Unlimited Power, Anthony Robbins
Property Secrets, Rob Moore
Be Obsessed or Be Average, Grant Cardone
Awaken the Giant Within, Anthony Robbins
Eat That Frog! Brian Tracy
Boost Your Pension and Income from Property, Kam Dovedi
The 4-Hour Work Week, Timothy Ferriss
Secrets of the Millionaire Mind, T. Harv Eker
Rich Dad Poor Dad, Robert Kiyosaki
Multiple Streams of Property Income, Rob Moore
Unshakable, Tony Robbins
The Miracle Morning, Hal Elrod
Life Leverage, Rob Moore
Finding My Virginity, Richard Branson
The 10X Rule, Grant Cardone
Elon Musk, Ashlee Vance
You Were Born Rich, Bob Proctor
Rich Dad's Cashflow Quadrant, Robert Kiyosaki
The Warren Buffet Way, Robert Hagstrom
The ABC's of Real Estate Investing, Ken McElroy
It's Not About the Money, Bob Proctor
Increase Your Financial IQ, Robert Kiyosaki
Tax Free Wealth, Tom Wheelwright
The Real Book of Real Estate, Robert Kiyosaki

The Mindset of a Millionaire, Bob Proctor
Multiple Streams of Property Income, Rob Moore
Culture Shift and Paradigms, Bob Proctor

About the Authors

Danny and Jo Phillips are a husband and wife dynamic duo. Together, they have created Phillips Real Estate Ltd., a property investing business, and have started developing their own property portfolio. In their first 12 months, they have bought a number of buy to let properties, and they have now progressed into commercial to residential conversion HMOs, and are joint venturing for development projects.

Jo Phillips is the visionary and creative side of the business. Using her analytical ability, she enjoys the research, and creating systems. Jo had an 8-year career as a police officer in the Metropolitan Police Service, London, UK, before changing direction. After graduating with a Masters of Art, from Camberwell University of the Arts, London, she created her own greeting card company. After great recognition and having her cards sold in the top London, Oxford Street department store, John Lewis, she successfully sold the business to a competitor.

Danny Phillips enjoyed a 35-year career as a police officer in the Metropolitan Police Service, London, UK. He had a number of diverse roles within the police, including being a front line operational officer, Family Liaison Officer, recruitment specialist, public speaker, and police trainer. During this time, he achieved Qualified Teacher Learning & Skills status. Danny is also a qualified lifeguard trainer and swimming teacher. He is the owner of FAB Training, a first aid training company, that supplies training all over the UK. www.fabtraining.org.uk

Danny and Jo are extremely dedicated in learning about the property world, and have a wealth of skills to implement into Phillips Real Estate

Ltd., and into their joint ventures. As this relatively new business blossoms, they are excited as to what the future holds, and they look forward to being able to help those just starting out on their property journey.